A YEAR OF

Pebble Go

# CONNECTING
## CONTENT TO LITERACY

BY KAREN ALEO

FOREWORD BY SHANNON MCCLINTOCK MILLER

MAUPIN HOUSE BY
CAPSTONE PROFESSIONAL
a capstone imprint

*A Year of PebbleGo®: Connecting Content to Literacy*
by Karen Aleo

Cover Design: Russell Griesmer
Interior Design: Lisa King
Editor: Emily Raij
Media Researcher: Kelly Garvin
Production Specialist: Kathy McColley

**Library of Congress Cataloging-in-Publication Data**
Library of Congress Cataloging-in-Publication data is available on the Library of Congress website.
978-1-4966-1801-6 (paperback)

**Image Credits:**
Photo by Justin Aleo, backcover; Shutterstock: bioraven, 95, Fine Art, 61, Monkey Business Images, inside backcover, Phonix_a Pk.sarote, cover and title page, Tyler Olson, inside backcover, Voin_Sveta, 13

Maupin House publishes professional resources for K–12 educators.
Visit www.capstonepd.com for free lesson plan downloads.

This book includes websites that were operational at the time it went to press.

Maupin House Publishing, Inc. by Capstone Professional
1710 Roe Crest Drive
North Mankato, MN 56003
www.capstonepd.com
888-262-6135
info@capstonepd.com

# CONTENTS

# Foreword

Friends, guess what? I have just the book for you that will be your favorite go-to resource for engaging your learners, while building content knowledge schoolwide!

It is *A Year of PebbleGo: Connecting Content to Literacy!*

I saw the difference that PebbleGo brings to a community as a K–12 teacher librarian. It was one of the digital databases I would visit every day as I planned, collaborated, and taught within the library and classrooms. And it was that one resource that hooked every single one of our students, teachers, and families!

However, this didn't happen by itself. I had to think creatively and work hard at making PebbleGo the go-to tool for all of our learning, research, and creative needs. And along the way, it became that place our students just loved to go to feed their curiosity and passion for so many amazing topics from animals, science, social studies, famous people, dinosaurs, and so much more!

Now there's a resource that supports educators and librarians as they introduce PebbleGo into the classroom and library. Not only does it provide a bridge between content and comprehension but it also includes ideas for research! This resource connects the library, classroom, and school in a collaborative and creative way.

*A Year of PebbleGo* provides 52 lessons that are to be used with PebbleGo. The lessons explain which article to use from the database. Then they lead you through suggestions for introducing the content to students as well as ideas for promoting comprehension of the article. In addition, the lessons support vocabulary acquisition. One of the key components of comprehension is vocabulary knowledge, so the lessons include key strategy support for building content vocabulary.

Two of the coolest things about this resource are that it connects to the curriculum and each lesson is titled with a question to encourage research! The lessons in this resource were mapped to state and national standards, so you know you are meeting the requirements by implementing the lessons. And the lessons hook students with questions such as Why do we need to know the weather? and Why do we need money? After students learn the content by way of the PebbleGo article, they can research these questions collaboratively and creatively to show what they learned. Most lessons include ideas for a research project!

With *A Year of PebbleGo*, you have the lessons needed to introduce the PebbleGo database. It is a one-stop resource for instruction, research ideas, differentiation support, and more! The next time you're wondering how to incorporate PebbleGo into your classroom, look no further than *A Year of PebbleGo!* It truly has everything that you are looking for to support comprehension, build content knowledge, and engage students in creative and exciting ways.

Not to mention, using PebbleGo is so much fun. I can't wait to use *A Year of PebbleGo* with my teachers and students!

**Shannon McClintock Miller**

K–12 Teacher Librarian
Speaker, Consultant, and Author

# Introduction

Children are naturally curious. They are beginning to understand the world around them and have questions about it. They come to the classroom or the library with these questions, providing a perfect opportunity to build on their curiosity with new knowledge. *A Year of PebbleGo: Connecting Content to Literacy* can help on this quest for knowledge.

PebbleGo is an award-winning K–2 database for reading and research. PebbleGo offers many database categories that make learning and improving reading and research skills fun while building on children's interests. These databases include PebbleGo Animals, PebbleGo Science, PebbleGo Biographies, PebbleGo Social Studies, PebbleGo Dinosaurs, and databases of the articles in Spanish. Each category includes many nonfiction articles that are filled with facts. Articles are easy to navigate and offer key reading supports such as read-along audio and word-by-word highlighting.

*A Year of PebbleGo* provides 52 lessons that are to be used with PebbleGo. This resource provides a step-by-step guide on how to integrate PebbleGo into the classroom or library. It taps into children's natural curiosity as each lesson begins with a question that could be answered with further research. At the beginning of each lesson, there is an opportunity to dive deep into the content, as the teacher or librarian provides enough background knowledge to pique interest and give students the information they need to prepare them for the article. While the lessons are scripted, it will be important for educators to adjust the lesson to match student ability level, interest, and need.

*A Year of PebbleGo* was crafted with inquiry in mind, building on the key skills of critical and creative thinking. The lessons can be dipped in and out of or used during the course of the year.

# The lessons

A *Year of PebbleGo* is divided into three sections. Lessons are based on content that is commonly taught at the emergent levels. Here is a breakdown of the kinds of lessons in *A Year of PebbleGo*:

➪ Science Lessons (pp. 13–59): Lessons in this section are tied to the Next Generation Science Standards (NGSS), Career and College Readiness Anchor Standards, and the American Association of School Librarians (AASL) Standards Framework for Learners. Instruction is centered on science content and comprehension of that content. Project-based learning activities within many of the lessons provide students with the opportunity to experiment with the world around them.

➪ Social Studies Lessons (pp. 61–94): Lessons in this section are tied to state standards, Career and College Readiness Anchor Standards, and the AASL Standards Framework for Learners. Instruction is centered on social studies content and comprehension of that content. Project-based learning activities within many of the lessons provide students with the opportunity to learn about the past and the present and to make connections to their world.

➪ Comprehension Lessons (pp. 95–113): Lessons in this section are tied to Career and College Readiness Anchor Standards and the AASL Standards Framework for Learners. Lessons provide support in comprehension strategies that lead to reading success: using prior knowledge, making connections, making predictions, clarifying/monitoring, questioning, visualizing, inferring, summarizing, and evaluating.

The science and social studies sections include two types of lessons. Most lessons are two pages and link content to literacy with the use of PebbleGo. Lessons provide an introduction to promote background knowledge on the topic of study, vocabulary strategy support, comprehension support, and practice to be completed collaboratively. The **Collaborative practice** gives students the opportunity to work within a group setting on project-based learning. **Differentiation** instruction rounds out the lesson, providing an extra layer of support for students of varying abilities. For an example of this type of lesson, see pages 14–15: **What are the steps in an experiment?** The second type of lesson provides support on how to use PebbleGo. The lesson identifies the features of the article. A question is provided as the lesson title, should educators wish to expand the lesson into project-based learning. For an example of this type of lesson, see page 66: **Who was Pocahontas?**

The comprehension lessons follow a gradual release of responsibility model, so learning moves toward independent takeover by students. Lessons provide a brief explanation of the strategy. Lessons then provide a model of the strategy with a PebbleGo article. There is a script with a suggestion for modeling the lesson for students. Teacher talk is in italics. This may be adjusted as needed. The lesson moves on to guided support, in which students are led to trying out the strategy with the article. Students practice the strategy collaboratively and then independently using the text. The lesson ends with an opportunity to extend the learning. For an example of this type of lesson, see pages 102–103: **Clarifying/Monitoring.**

To strengthen the learning and promote recall, content and comprehension lessons include an opportunity to take notes. Lessons reference graphic organizers (pp. 114–124) and include tips at point of use on how to use the graphic organizers for note-taking. As many of the articles on PebbleGo include a Spanish counterpart, Spanish translations of the graphic organizers are available at the website for *A Year of PebbleGo*.

## How to use *A Year of PebbleGo*

*A Year of PebbleGo* provides robust lessons that connect students to grade-appropriate content and literacy skills and strategies. The lessons can be used to supplement instruction or to regularly practice strategy use with PebbleGo. With continued practice, students will likely surprise educators with their own wonderings. PebbleGo includes many articles on topics of interest, providing opportunities for students to do further research.

## A note about Internet safety

It sometimes seems that before children learn to talk, they are able to toggle between apps on a smartphone and know what each app is for. Children are learning early just how to get information. When it comes to research, the best practice is for teachers or librarians to view outside websites or books before students are permitted to use them on their own. Discuss Internet safety tips with students to ensure safe practices, and supervise them so they are using sources properly.

# Empowering learning

PebbleGo articles have a number of features to engage students while building content knowledge. Articles can be read by students or read to them. And a variety of supports are provided to reinforce concepts—from videos to activities for hands-on learning to opportunities for students to share what they know.

As students read the articles, they'll likely discuss their wonderings with each other. Take these questions as opportunities for future research. For example, an article about a famous author, such as Dr. Seuss, may lead students to want to read books by Theodor Seuss Geisel or learn more about when Geisel lived.

*A Year of PebbleGo* provides many opportunities to empower learning. Six ideas are discussed here that can fit into the curriculum and classroom.

1) *Encourage students to share out during the lesson.* Quiet classrooms are a thing of the past, and students learn when they feel safe sharing their thoughts. PebbleGo lessons have been set up to promote discussion.

2) *Discuss learning goals with students.* Many of the lessons include projects offering choice in research. Discuss interests with students so they feel empowered to work on projects that are of importance to them.

3) *Encourage students to use technology in a way that improves their learning.* Depending on the students' level, they may read the article or have the article read to them. If students are unable to read the article due to level, or if students are unclear what an academic vocabulary word means, encourage them to use the PebbleGo features in a way that makes the most sense to them. For some students, that may mean having the entire article read to them. For others, it might mean allowing them to use the glossary resource so unknown words are understood right away. By allowing them to troubleshoot issues on their own, they are learning how to monitor their reading.

4) *Allow students to conduct research based on their own wonderings.* As students are led through PebbleGo experiences, they are likely to have new questions that can be answered with further research. Encourage students to find the answers to their questions with additional PebbleGo articles or books. Lessons with project-based learning opportunities provide ideas in the **Further research** section.

5) *Encourage various ways to demonstrate learning.* Many content lessons include a suggestion for a final product. Allow students choice in the matter. For example, if the product is to complete a Venn diagram comparing two classifications of animals, allow students to share this information in another way. Perhaps the student wants to make a collage instead and explain why he or she chose certain pictures.

6) *Post student questions and products.* Show pride in students' learning by posting their projects and wonderings. *A Year of PebbleGo* is filled with questions that promote new findings, but these questions don't end after research. Encourage students to share their questions and post them around the room. Have students conduct research to find new answers.

# Setting up for *A Year of PebbleGo*

Setting up the room for online learning may be one of the trickiest parts to having students work with the database. With a few rules in place, students will be ready to go.

Begin by setting expectations for the time together. Explain that the time with PebbleGo is not playtime, but an opportunity to learn. Depending on whether students are using the database with a tablet or in a computer lab, there may be additional rules to discuss with students. These might include how to line up to go to the lab, where to find the tablet and how to power it up, and so on.

Then give a warm-up, explaining how to use the database. Educators may either set up the page for students or go over how to do it. Student volunteers could be called upon to help others find the article. Note that each lesson identifies which article will be used in the **Materials** section. After logging into PebbleGo, enter the name of the article in the search bar to find it.

Provide time for students to explore an article. Go over the main features, and explain that each article has different sections. The sections of the article are located in the tabs at the top, and each tab provides new information related to the article.

The toolbars at the bottom of the page include the article and images, activity worksheets, and videos. Depending on student ability, educators may want to have students focus on the article only and not the toolbars. Educators can use the toolbars to print out materials for students to work on in centers. If technology resources are limited, copies of the article could be printed out for students to work on during the lesson.

Consider coming up with a list of rules for this time together. Explain what is to happen at this time, and work together to draft an anchor chart with expectations. A little work up front will help ensure students are on task and engaged during the lessons.

# Building knowledge

S tudents may come to the classroom with limited knowledge about a particular topic. For example, if the lesson is about force and what it is used for, and students don't know some of the concepts that will be discussed, preteaching the content may become necessary.

*A Year of PebbleGo* provides the support needed to build this knowledge and prepare students to read the article. Content lessons start with an **Introduce the topic** section. The educator prompts students to think about the topic and share what they already know, thus giving students an opportunity to activate their prior knowledge. Lessons may also include some background knowledge so students will be ready to read the article. Like the content lessons, the comprehension lessons include a warm-up. The educator defines the strategy and then jumps into the article, modeling the strategy right away. Because it will be important to have students dive into the article, adjust the amount of time needed to introduce the topic.

## Technology standards

The International Society for Technology in Education (ISTE) has created standards to support students in today's changing technological world. One of the ISTE Standards for Students (2016) is Knowledge Constructor, and according to the standard, students are to review different types of resources, including digital tools, and synthesize knowledge. They are also to make the research process a meaningful one, such as by way of a product.

Meeting this particular standard could be a tall order for the early elementary student. But it is possible to support this standard in a way that is developmentally appropriate and meaningful to young students. *A Year of PebbleGo* does just that.

Content lessons encourage students to try out the database individually or collaboratively. Students can go a little deeper into the content by reading additional articles or books on the subject. A section of the lesson called **Further research** lists articles and books related to the content. Students also utilize these resources and classroom discourse to work on a project. Students often choose certain aspects of the project to focus on, thus increasing engagement.

## Active participation

When students are actively involved in the learning, they are better able to build knowledge and retain information. The lessons provide several opportunities for students to be involved in their learning.

- *Note-taking: A Year of PebbleGo* includes 10 graphic organizers (pp. 114–124) that can be reproduced for students. Content and comprehension lessons reference a graphic organizer for taking notes. As students are learning about the content or the strategy, they use the graphic organizer to keep track of new learning or evidence from the text. Students can then use these notes for project-based assignments or for recall of important details.

- *Discussion:* Throughout the lessons, educators ask students questions to build discussion—such as when they introduce the topic, ask comprehension questions, or help support dialogue during collaborative practice.

- *Collaborative practice:* Each content lesson includes **Collaborative practice**, which gives students the opportunity to work on a project that is related to the content in some way. Through this practice, students learn important lessons about working in a group.

- *Independent work:* Comprehension lessons include opportunities for students to try out the strategy on their own. Students use the graphic organizer to show their understanding of the strategy.

Lessons provide other opportunities for active participation, such as through vocabulary work or sharing their work. Educators may also find additional ways to bring active participation to the forefront. In doing so, students take on responsibility for their learning.

Building knowledge doesn't end when the PebbleGo lesson wraps up. The goal is for students to remember these lessons and the comprehension strategy supports as they continue to grow their content knowledge in the future.

# Collaboration

It takes time for students to develop the skills needed to collaborate successfully in groups. And yet the ability to collaborate is something that students need to be able to do in order to be successful in school and their careers. Collaboration is gaining more importance, especially among standards. Teaching young students the skills needed to collaborate early can help them be successful during group work.

Every educator handles things a little differently, and the approach discussed here could be adjusted to meet student needs. To begin, consider coming up with a list of rules for collaborative work and posting that list. A few ideas for this list include the following: 1) Give the speaker your full attention; 2) Only one person speaks at a time; 3) Raise your hand if you'd like to add to a comment (adjust this rule to whatever your preferred method is); 4) Give positive comments; 5) State disagreements politely and with evidence; and so on. Educators and their students will likely come up with additional rules that meet the needs of the class or group.

## Listening skills

Listening while another student is speaking is a skill that can be a challenge but one that all young students need to learn early on. Let students know the importance of everyone having the opportunity to share his or her thoughts. A helpful tool for young children is to give them a number. Explain if a student just shared something, that student should wait until a certain number of students share before speaking again.

Listening skills are especially important when students are working away from the teacher. There may be one or two children who want to dominate the conversation and the work. Remind students to allow a wait time so that others can be part of the work. Providing roles during group work will also help. Some of the lessons identify tasks that could be divvied up by team member.

## Collaboration as routine

Collaboration time is a routine, and like all routines, it should be practiced. Model the skill and allow plenty of time for students to practice it. Taking time out for students to work on this skill with meaningful tasks will help them learn the expectations and how to work with others successfully.

# Differentiation

No two children are the same, nor should they be taught in the same way. Because everyone learns at a different pace, instruction should be adjusted to meet student needs. Differentiation is instruction that is altered to meet the needs of students with the goal of having all students become lifelong learners.

There are different ways to differentiate. Differentiation occurs whenever delivery of content is adjusted, the process in making meaning is amended, or the product showing evidence of learning is changed to match the need of the learner. We provide an explanation of each method.

## Content

Content is differentiated when the way information is delivered is adjusted for the end user. Sometimes this is by level. For example, teachers and librarians may have a few books about a given topic written at different levels. Other times, the content is provided electronically and the text is read to students. PebbleGo content is provided in this manner. Each article includes a speaker button. Students either can read the article on their own or have the article read to them by clicking on the speaker button. When activating the button, the text is highlighted word for word and read aloud. The speaker function also appears when students click on academic terms highlighted in red. Content can be further adjusted through book buddies with one student reading to another. Assessments can help determine student level.

## Process

Students make sense of information in different ways. Some are able to grasp information right away, while others need more time. This difference may be due to learning style, lack of prior knowledge about the content, or simply just how students prefer to take in new content. One way to adjust process is to provide more time as needed. Here are other ways that process can be changed to meet student needs:

⇨ Offer additional scaffolding (vocabulary, comprehension, etc.) to those students requiring more help. One way to support students with vocabulary is to provide a list of words with image supports.

⇨ Group students by ability; this grouping should be flexible so students can be regrouped.

⇨ Offer students the opportunity to use different ways of making meaning. For example, provide a different type of graphic organizer to take notes or adjust an activity for students.

Content lessons in this resource include a section on differentiation. The **Differentiation** section often identifies how to adjust the lesson for process.

# Product

Educators can also differentiate the product. Each content lesson includes an opportunity for project-based learning. When adjusting the product, work with students to get a better understanding of what they are able to do, and perhaps more important, what they would like to do. If they are working on a project they feel excited about, they will be more engaged and willing to put in extra effort.

Another way to adjust the product is to modify how it is done. Some students will require a little more support while others would like to work in smaller groups. Keep these considerations in mind while creating groups or partnerships for **Collaborative practice**.

# Other considerations

When it comes to differentiation, it is important to take into account three additional areas: student readiness, interest, and learning profile. Readiness is the ability to work on a topic or skill at a particular time. Two ways to adjust for readiness are to provide more background support and to provide direct instruction in small groups. Interest is taken into account when there is student choice in instruction—whether that is how the content is delivered or how students choose to complete products. Giving students the opportunity to share their interests can help educators glean this information. Lastly, educators can adjust the lessons by learning profile when each student's unique ability to learn is considered. Flexibility in environment, grouping, and modes of how the instruction is delivered (i.e., auditory, visual, and kinesthetic) are some of the ways to adjust instruction for learning profile.

# Getting started

Ayear of fun, learning, and inspiration is ahead. Students will learn about how animals survive, where light comes from, who helped to shape the United States, and much more. Learning about these topics will open the door to collaboration, discussion, research, and new wonderings. And building comprehension strategies will give students the tools they need to be successful readers.

When deciding which lesson with which to begin, compare the Table of Contents to the curriculum. Select topics that supplement the science and social studies work students will be exploring, correspond with the comprehension strategy work from the core curriculum, or help celebrate special days of the year.

*A Year of PebbleGo* includes 52 lessons. A typical lesson may take around 30–40 minutes, and the collaborative project could be completed during the week. Instruction time should be adjusted as needed. The majority of the time should be spent on having students read the article, so time spent on introducing the topic could be reduced.

As mentioned previously, build in time prior to working on the lessons to practice working collaboratively. Students will need to know what the expectations are during this time. Co-constructing an anchor chart will help support the purpose of collaborative work and remind students of what to do.

We hope *A Year of PebbleGo* will help young learners get excited about the PebbleGo database. While working on the lessons, take note of what has been working well. As we are always interested in hearing how educators are using PebbleGo, we welcome you to share ideas at the Capstone Community webpage at https://community.mycapstone.com. This website provides the opportunity to not only share new ideas with Capstone but to share and discover new ways of using PebbleGo with other users. We hope this product serves you well, and we look forward to hearing from you.

## References

1. American Association of School Librarians. 2018. *National School Library Standards for Learners, School Librarians, and School Libraries.* ALA: Chicago.

2. International Society for Technology in Education. 2016. *ISTE Standards for Students.* Retrieved from www.iste.org/standards.

3. National Governors Association Center for Best Practices, Council of Chief State School Officers. 2010. *Common Core State Standards for English Language Arts.* National Governors Association Center for Best Practices, Council of Chief State School Officers: Washington, D.C.

4. NGSS Lead States. 2013. *Next Generation Science Standards.* The National Academies Press: Washington, D.C.

# Science Lessons

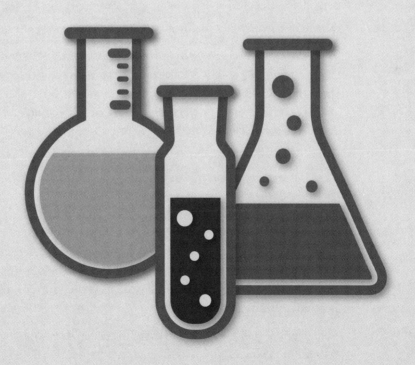

# What are the steps in an experiment?

## Introduce the topic

*Who can tell me what an experiment is? Why do scientists do experiments?* (Allow time for student responses. They may say that an experiment is something scientists do to test something they have a question about.)

*Science does not begin with the experiment. It begins with an observation, or something the scientist saw and noticed. For example, maybe the scientist noticed a buoy floating in the water. He or she might question why it floats and come up with a best guess about it. Maybe the scientist thinks the buoy is lighter than the water. Then the scientist will conduct, or do, an experiment to test that guess.*

*In this lesson, we are going to learn more about what the steps are to an experiment. Then we will take what we learn to come up with the steps to our own experiment. To begin, let's fill in a KWL Chart. We will use the KWL Chart to take notes before, during, and after we read the PebbleGo article. Taking notes is a helpful way to keep track of what we know and learn. We can use our notes later when we draft the steps to an experiment.*

*What do we already know about the steps in an experiment? Let's write what we know in the first column.* (Model for students, such as noticing that scientists always begin with a question they have. Then take some time to write student responses in the first column.) *What do we want to know about the steps to an experiment? Let's write what we want to know in the second column.* (Model for students, such as asking how scientists come up with their questions. Then take some time to write student responses in the second column.)

*Today we are going to read the PebbleGo article "Let's Investigate." As we read, let's fill in the final column with what we learned.*

Depending on the level of support needed, have students read or listen to the article, or read the article to students. The instruction that follows will help to support comprehension of the content as well as connect students to the science topic.

# Vocabulary support

Be on the lookout for vocabulary words that students do not know. Encourage students to share these words with the class. The following is a model on context clues and can be completed with many of the terms.

*Some of you had asked me what "object" means. (From Observations) Let's take a closer look at the sentence it is in to see if there is a clue, or hint, to its meaning. The sentence says, "Look closely at an object." Are there some clues that will help us figure out the word "object"? The author is asking us to look closely at an object. In order to look at it, it has to be something we can see. What do you think the word "object" means based on this clue?* (Wait for student responses.) *That's right, an object must be something we can see. By looking it up in the dictionary, I learned an object is something that can be seen or touched.*

Have students take notes on other words that cause confusion. Explain that by clicking on the words in red, students can get a quick definition.

# Comprehension support

⇨ *What is an investigation?* (It is a test used to find answers to a question.) *Let's write our answers in the third column of the KWL Chart.*

⇨ *What are the steps to an experiment?* (Provide support as needed to help students with the steps to an experiment. They include: observation, question, best guess, experiment, answer.) *Where in the article did you find the answers to this question?* (Steps in an Experiment)

⇨ *Let's review the KWL Chart. What did we know before we read the article? What did we learn?* (Acknowledge and accept student responses.)

# Collaborative practice ✐

Have students work in groups to reread the article and come up with their own experiment. Encourage students to think of something they've wondered about and how they might be able to test it. If students are unsure, consider providing a few examples, such as what can sink or float or what kinds of patterns will appear on paper by rubbing over different objects with pencil. Encourage students to work in their groups to draft the steps of an experiment and to try it. For further practice, try the activity as a class. Click on the paper and crayon icon in the "Let's Investigate" article, find Activity, and click on Print.

## Differentiation

Encourage students to read additional information on the topic, using ideas from **Further research** below. Consider pairing different learning types together, so that one student might help another. For learners who might require more support, use the article's format as a guide. The article is naturally grouped, or chunked, by topic. Review each tab with students and ask them leading questions prior to moving on to the next tab. Use the pictures to reinforce concepts.

## Further research

- PebbleGo "Asking Questions"
- PebbleGo "Answers and Solutions"
- Rompella, Natalie. *Experiments in Light and Sound with Toys and Everyday Stuff.* Fun Science. North Mankato, Minn.: Capstone Press, 2016.

# Why are the five senses important?

## Toolbars

There is a toolbar of related resources that can be printed (Print toolbar) and another that can be viewed (Media toolbar).

### Print

> Cite icon (pencil and paper): Students may need to reference the article should they be writing a report. They can click on this icon to see the citation as well as highlight it, copy it, and paste it into their report. The citation can also be printed out, placed at learning centers, and used as a reference.

> Article icon (papers): If you'd like to have a printout of the article or the images for center work, click on this icon. Either or both can be printed out.

> Activities icon (crayon and paper): The "Hearing" article includes a Share what you know activity. You can print this out for students to work on. Consider placing it at a center, and encourage students to work collaboratively on the activity. Other activities include a Life Sciences: Hearing Activity, which is an experiment on hearing, and a Questions for Understanding worksheet.

### Media

> Video icon (TV): Before or after reading the article, encourage students to watch the videos for more information about hearing. There are two videos in this section.

Each PebbleGo article has many resources that will help encourage learning about the topic. This lesson explores the resources that appear in the "Hearing" article. Encourage students to review these assets in order to answer the question, "Why are the five senses important?" The format of this lesson may be used to introduce most PebbleGo articles. Some articles may have different asset types.

## Article features

Articles have a number of features that you will want to go over with students.

> Each article provides content by tabs, with each tab on one main idea. With "Hearing," there is a tab on What Is Hearing?, What You Hear, How You Hear, Messages to Your Brain, and Why You Hear. An activity on exploring main idea and details would be a perfect way to introduce the tabs to students.

> Students can read the article or have it read to them by clicking on the speaker icon.

> Academic terms are highlighted in red. By clicking on the word and the speaker icon, students can read and hear a glossary definition of the word.

> Each tab includes a picture that supports the text.

> The related articles for "Hearing" can be seen by doing a search on Senses. These articles include "Seeing," "Smelling," "Tasting," and "Touching" and will be helpful as students answer the question, "Why are the five senses important?"

## Standards

NGSS: 1-PS4-1

**College and Career Readiness Standards:**
CCSS.ELA-Literacy.CCRA.R.7, CCSS.ELA-Literacy.CCRA.R.9

**AASL Standards Framework for Learners:**
I.A.2, I.D.3, VI.A.1

## Materials

- "Hearing" PebbleGo article

# What is matter?

## Introduce the topic

*Look around you. Everything is made of matter. What do you think matter is?*
(Allow time for student responses. Consider taking notes on a whiteboard as students call out their responses.)

*I heard you say that matter is all around us, and some of you listed things in the classroom. Did you know that we are matter too? That's right! We are matter and everything around us is matter. Matter can be a solid. Who can tell me what a solid is?* (Encourage student responses.) *That's right—a solid is something that you can see and that you can touch. It has a shape and size. But did you know that matter has three states? The solid state is just one of them.*

*In this lesson, we are going to learn more about what is matter. Then we will take what we learn to come up with an experiment on matter. To begin, let's fill in a Three Column Chart. We will use this chart to take notes before and after we read the PebbleGo article. Taking notes is a helpful way to keep track of what we know and learn. We can use our notes later when we draft the steps to an experiment.*

*In the first column, we are going to write down the title Solids. What kinds of things should we include in the solids part of the chart?* (Model for students, such as the pen or chalk you are using to write. Then take some time to write student responses in the first column.) *In the next column, we are going to write down Liquids. That is another state of matter. What kinds of liquids should we include in this part of the chart?* (Take some time to write student responses in the second column.) *Our final column is going to be labeled Gases. What is a gas? What kinds of things are gases?* (Encourage student responses, but don't go too deep in discussion, so students may read about the three states of matter on their own and revise their thinking.)

*Today we are going to read the PebbleGo article "What Is Matter?" As we read, let's fill in the columns with what we learned.*

Depending on the level of support needed, have students read or listen to the article, or read the article to students. The instruction that follows will help to support comprehension of the content as well as connect students to the science topic.

## Vocabulary support

Be on the lookout for vocabulary words that students do not know. Encourage students to share these words with the class. The following is a model on context clues and can be completed with many of the terms.

### Standards

**NGSS:**
2-PS1-1, 2-PS1-2

**College and Career Readiness Standards:**
CCSS.ELA-Literacy.CCRA.R.1,
CCSS.ELA-Literacy.CCRA.R.4,
CCSS.ELA-Literacy.CCRA.L.4,
CCSS.ELA-Literacy.CCRA.L.6

**AASL Standards Framework for Learners:**
I.A.1, I.A.2, I.B.1, I.D.3, III.D.1, V.C.2, VI.A.1

### Materials

- "What Is Matter?" PebbleGo article
- Three Column Chart, p. 115

## Differentiation

Encourage students to work through the experiment by pairing different learning types together, so that one student might help another. For learners who might require more support, go over the vocabulary with them. The article has a lot of academic vocabulary, and students could benefit from further support on the terms. Connecting the photos to the terms will also help. Then review each tab with students and ask them leading questions prior to moving on to the next tab.

## Further research

- PebbleGo Materials articles
- PebbleGo "Properties of Materials"
- Braun, Eric. *Curious Pearl Explains States of Matter: 4D An Augmented Reality Science Experience*. Curious Pearl, Science Girl 4D. North Mankato, Minn.: Picture Window Books, 2018.

*Someone had asked what the word "property" has to do with the states of matter. (From Solids) Let's take a closer look at the sentence it is in to see if there is a clue, or hint, to its meaning. The sentence says, "A property of a rock is its color." Are there some clues that will help us figure out the word "property"? The author is telling us that color is one property. I'm still not sure what the meaning is, so I am going to read on. The author then gives examples of other features of a rock—like it's hardness. I think property has to do with its features. I'm going to click on the word because the red color lets me know the word is linked to a glossary definition. By seeing the definition, I learn that "property" is a "quality in a material, like color, hardness, or shape." Using context clues, or hints around the word, and the glossary helped me figure out the meaning of property.*

Have students take notes on other words that cause confusion. Explain that by clicking on the words in red, students can get a quick definition.

## Comprehension support

⟳ *What is the most important information about solids?* (They are able to keep their shape and size.) *The article lists some examples of solids. Are there any we can add to or chart? Are there others we didn't think of? Let's write our answers in the first column of our chart.*

⟳ *How are liquids and gases the same? How are they different?* (Liquids and gases both do not have a shape. Some liquids are safe to touch whereas gases cannot be felt, unless it's windy.) *Where in the article did you find the answers to these questions? Or did you need to make an inference, or use what you already knew with the information in the article to come up with this conclusion?* (Liquids, Solids, and inference)

⟳ *Let's review the Three Column Chart. What did we know before we read the article? What did we learn?* (Acknowledge and accept student responses.)

## Collaborative practice ✎

Have students work in groups to reread the article and come up with their own experiment. Encourage students to think of something they've wondered about with regards to matter and how they might be able to test it. There may be some limitations as to how students can test the difference between a solid, liquid, and gas. If students need help, consider having them start by comparing and contrasting the three states of matter. Provide them with three containers. In the first, they put objects. In the second, they put a liquid, such as water, and the third they keep empty. Encourage students to compare and contrast the properties in each of the containers. Then ask students, how they can make the liquid a solid or a gas—what would need to happen? For further practice, try the activity as a class. Click on the paper and crayon icon in the "What Is Matter?" article, find Activity, and click on Print.

# What is force used for?

**Standards**

NGSS:
K-PS2-1, K-PS2-2

**College and Career Readiness Standards:**
CCSS.ELA-Literacy.CCRA.R.1,
CCSS.ELA-Literacy.CCRA.R.2,
CCSS.ELA-Literacy.CCRA.R.4,
CCSS.ELA-Literacy.CCRA.R.9,
CCSS.ELA-Literacy.CCRA.W.7,
CCSS.ELA-Literacy.CCRA.L.4,
CCSS.ELA-Literacy.CCRA.L.6

**AASL Standards Framework for Learners:**
I.A.1, I.A.2, I.D.1, III.B.1, III.D.1, VI.A.1

**Materials**

- "Kinds of Forces" PebbleGo article
- T-Chart, p. 117

## Introduce the topic

*For something to move, it needs some sort of force on it. A force is a power that causes something else to change or move. What is one type of force that you know about? When is it used?* (Allow time for student responses. If students do not know the answer to this question, direct them to think about pushes and pulls—asking what a push or a pull can do.)

*I heard some of you say a push is one kind of force, and someone might push a cart in a grocery store. Where else have you seen pushes being used? What about pulls?* (Encourage student responses.) *We've seen pushes and pulls all over—from someone pushing a ball to someone pulling or pushing open a door.*

*In this lesson, we are going to learn more about force and when different types of forces are used. Then we will take what we learn to write about one type of force. To begin, let's fill in a T-Chart. We will use this chart to take notes before and after we read the PebbleGo article. Taking notes is a helpful way to keep track of what we know and learn. We can use our notes later when we do a little more research on a force and what it's used for.*

*Let's write a title for the first column. We are going to write the title Type of Force. We'll label the second column When It's Used. We've already started talking about pushes and pulls, so let's add those forces to our chart. What should we put in the second column for each force?* (Model for students, such as pulling a wagon and pushing a door. Then take some time to write student responses in the T-Chart.)

*Today we are going to read the PebbleGo article "Kinds of Forces." As we read, let's fill in the columns with what we learned.*

Depending on the level of support needed, have students read or listen to the article, or read the article to students. The instruction that follows will help to support comprehension of the content as well as connect students to the science topic.

## Vocabulary support

Be on the lookout for vocabulary words that students do not know. Encourage students to share these words with the class. Some of the words include a definition within the sentence, which might be a helpful lesson for students.

**Further research**

- PebbleGo "What Is Motion?"
- PebbleGo "Gravity"
- PebbleGo "Friction"
- Royston, Angela. *All About Forces.* All About Science. Chicago: Heinemann Library, 2016.

*I noticed some of you are not sure what the word "friction" means. (From Number) Let's take a closer look at the sentence it is in to see if there is a clue, or hint, to its meaning. The sentence says, "Friction is a force that slows down objects when they rub together." It sounds like the author is giving us a definition of the word within the sentence. The author gives the word and then says what the word means. I noticed when I clicked on the word "friction" and saw the definition, it was the same as the sentence. Authors sometimes explain a word by including the definition in the sentence. Have you noticed this with other words in the article? Which ones? Why do you think authors sometimes put definitions of words right in the text?* (Acknowledge and accept student responses. They might say the words "force" and "gravity" include the definition in the article and that authors include definitions in the text to further explain something tricky.)

Have students take notes on other words that cause confusion. Explain that by clicking on the words in red, students can get a quick definition.

## Comprehension support

↪ *Why is the size of a force important?* (The size of the force is important for how far and how fast the object will go.) *Where did you find this information?* (in the tab labeled Size)

↪ *What kinds of forces did you learn about? Are there any kinds of forces and the things they do we can add to our T-Chart?* (Acknowledge and accept student responses.)

↪ *What did we learn about forces from reading this article? Where did you find the information about forces?* (Acknowledge and accept student responses.)

## Collaborative practice ✎

Have students work in groups to reread the article and come up with their own inquiry project for further research. Encourage students to think of a type of force they'd like to know more about, how it works, and what it's used for. If students need help, point to the T-Chart and review the forces and when they might occur. Students can use the resources listed in **Further research** or other library resources to research a force. Consider having students share what they've learned with the class.

For further study on the topic, try the activity as a class. Click on the paper and crayon icon in the "Kinds of Forces" article, find Activity, and click on Print.

# Why do things move the way they do?

## Standards

**NGSS:**
K-PS2-1, K-PS2-2

**College and Career Readiness Standards:**
CCSS.ELA-Literacy.CCRA.R.1,
CCSS.ELA-Literacy.CCRA.R.2,
CCSS.ELA-Literacy.CCRA.R.4,
CCSS.ELA-Literacy.CCRA.L.4,
CCSS.ELA-Literacy.CCRA.L.5,
CCSS.ELA-Literacy.CCRA.L.6

**AASL Standards Framework for Learners:**
I.A.1, I.A.2, I.B.1, I.D.2, III.D.1, V.C.2, VI.A.1

## Introduce the topic

This lesson works well by having students sit in a circle. Place one marble on the ground in the middle of the circle. Take a second marble and try to hit the marble in the middle of the circle with it.

*What happened to the marble when I hit it with a second marble?* (Students will likely say that the first marble was moved by the second marble.)

*We just saw motion in action. Sir Isaac Newton was a scientist in the 1600s. He came up with laws of motion. One law is that objects will be still unless something else changes them. Did this law happen with the marbles? How?* (Encourage and accept student responses.)

*This law also says an object in motion will keep going in the same direction and at the same speed unless something changes it. How did we see this law happen with the marbles?* (Encourage and accept student responses.)

*I heard some of you say that the marble was still until another marble hit it. And that the second marble lost some of its speed once it hit the marble in the center.*

*In this lesson, we are going to learn more about motion and why things move the way they do. Then we will take what we learn to do an experiment on motion. To begin, let's fill in a Venn diagram. We are going to write Motion as the title of the first circle. We are going to write Force as the title of the second circle. Force is a power that causes something to move or change. We are going to title the place where the two circles meet as Both. We are going to fill in the Venn diagram as we read the PebbleGo article. Taking notes is a helpful way to keep track of what we know and learn. We can use our notes later when we do an experiment on motion.*

*We've already started talking about motion. Are there any words we can add to Motion? What did the marbles do? What are some other motions you can think of?* (Model for students, such as rolling and spinning. Then take some time to write student responses in the Venn diagram.)

*Today we are going to read the PebbleGo article "What Is Motion?" As we read, let's fill in the Venn diagram with what we learned.*

## Materials

- "What Is Motion?" PebbleGo article
- Venn Diagram, p. 122
- Marbles

## Differentiation

For the **Collaborative practice**, encourage higher-level students to come up with different ways to alter the experiment for a different outcome, such as by using ramps or blockers. For learners who might require more support, it may be helpful to pair learners together and to provide them with more time. Be sure to provide coaching as requested.

## Further research

- PebbleGo "Kinds of Forces"
- PebbleGo "Gravity"
- PebbleGo "Friction"
- James, Emily. *The Simple Science of Motion*. Simply Science. North Mankato, Minn.: Capstone Press, 2018.

Depending on the level of support needed, have students read or listen to the article, or read the article to students. The instruction that follows will help to support comprehension of the content as well as connect students to the science topic.

# Vocabulary support

Be on the lookout for vocabulary words that students do not know. Encourage students to share these words with the class. Students can use strategies, such as searching for a synonym in close proximity to an unknown word, in order to understand the word's meaning.

*I noticed some of you were not sure what the word "distance" means.* (From Measuring Motion) *Let's take a closer look at the sentence it is in to see if there is a clue, or hint, to its meaning. The sentence says, "We can measure distance and speed." We don't know what the word means from that sentence, so let's look around that sentence for clues. The section starts with, "How far and fast did that car move?" I know that "fast" can be connected to the word "speed." If something is going really fast, it has speed. "Fast" is a synonym for "speed." A synonym means a word that is almost the same as another word. Sometimes it's helpful to try to find synonyms nearby a word you're not sure about. Is there a word in the first sentence that is a synonym for "distance"?* (Acknowledge and accept student responses.) *I heard some of you say "far" can be a synonym for "distance."*

Have students take notes on other words that cause confusion. Explain that by clicking on the words in red, students can get a quick definition.

# Comprehension support

⇨ *What did we learn about forces and motion?* (Forces can cause motion.) Where did you find this information? (in the tab labeled Motion and Force)

⇨ *How do forces cause motion? Is there anything we can add to our Venn diagram?* (Acknowledge and accept student responses. Students might say that pushes and pulls can cause motion.)

⇨ *What did we learn about motion from reading this article? Can we add information to our Venn diagram?* (Acknowledge and accept student responses.)

# Collaborative practice ✐

Have students work in groups to come up with an experiment on motion. Provide students with a few marbles. Students will come up with the steps to an experiment about how things move using the marbles. Through the completion of the experiment, they should be able to predict how marbles might move and to answer the inquiry question, "Why do things move the way they do?"

For further study on the topic, try the activity as a class. Click on the paper and crayon icon in the "What Is Motion?" article, find Activity, and click on Print.

# What is mass?

Each PebbleGo article has many resources that will help encourage learning about the topic. This lesson explores the resources that appear in the "Mass and Weight" article. Encourage students to review these assets in order to answer the question, "What is mass?" The format of this lesson may be used to introduce most PebbleGo articles. Some articles may have different asset types.

## Article features

Articles have a number of features that you will want to go over with students.

- ⤷ Each article provides content by tabs, with each tab on one main idea. With "Mass and Weight," there is a tab on What Is a Property?, Mass, Weight, How Mass Is Measured, and How Weight Is Measured. An activity on exploring main idea and details would be a perfect way to introduce the tabs to students.

- ⤷ Students can read the article or have it read to them by clicking on the speaker icon.

- ⤷ Academic terms are highlighted in red. By clicking on the word and the speaker icon, students can read and hear a glossary definition of the word.

- ⤷ Each tab includes a picture that supports the text.

- ⤷ The related articles for "Mass and Weight" can be seen by doing a search on Properties of Materials. These articles include "Density and Volume," "Floating and Sinking," and "Heavy or Light?" and will be helpful as students answer the question, "What is mass?"

### Standards

NGSS: 2-PS1-1

**College and Career Readiness Standards:**
CCSS.ELA-Literacy.CCRA.R.7,
CCSS.ELA-Literacy.CCRA.R.9

**AASL Standards Framework for Learners:**
I.A.2, I.D.3, VI.A.1

### Materials

- "Mass and Weight" PebbleGo article

## Toolbars

There is a toolbar of related resources that can be printed (Print toolbar) and another that can be viewed (Media toolbar).

### Print

> Cite icon (pencil and paper): Students may need to reference the article should they be writing a report. They can click on this icon to see the citation as well as highlight it, copy it, and paste it into their report. The citation can also be printed out, placed at learning centers, and used as a reference.

> Article icon (papers): If you'd like to have a printout of the article or the images for center work, click on this icon. Either or both can be printed out.

> Activities icon (crayon and paper): The "Mass and Weight" article includes a Share what you know activity. You can print this out for students to work on. Consider placing it at a center, and encourage students to work collaboratively on the activity. Other activities include a Physical Sciences: Mass and Weight activity, which is an experiment on mass, and a Questions for Understanding worksheet.

### Media

> Video icon (TV): Before or after reading the article, encourage students to watch the videos for more information about mass and weight. There are two videos in this section.

**Standards**

NGSS:
2-PS1-1, 2-PS1-2

**College and Career
Readiness Standards:**
CCSS.ELA-Literacy.CCRA.R.1,
CCSS.ELA-Literacy.CCRA.R.2,
CCSS.ELA-Literacy.CCRA.R.4,
CCSS.ELA-Literacy.CCRA.R.9,
CCSS.ELA-Literacy.CCRA.W.7,
CCSS.ELA-Literacy.CCRA.L.4,
CCSS.ELA-Literacy.CCRA.L.6

**AASL Standards
Framework for Learners:**
I.A.1, I.A.2, I.B.3, I.D.2, III.D.1,
IV.B.1, V.C.2, VI.A.1

**Materials**

- "Magnetism" PebbleGo
article
- Main Idea and Details Sheet,
p. 121

# Where are magnets found?

## Introduce the topic

*Did you ever play with letters that could stick to a refrigerator? How did the letters stick to the fridge? Magnets! A magnet is a special metal that can attract other metals to it. When it attracts other metals, it pulls the metals to it. That's how the letters you played with were able to stick to the fridge. The magnet attached to the letter was attracted to the metal in the fridge. Today, we are going to find out more about magnets and learn about all kinds of things that use magnets to work.*

*Let's start with a compass. Who knows what a compass is? When might a compass be used?* (Allow time for student responses. If students do not know the answer to this question, explain that a compass is a tool that always points north. It helps people find their way.)

*I heard some of you say a compass is a small tool with directions and a needle on it, and people might use a compass if they are lost in the woods. Did you know that a compass is a magnet? How it works is that Earth is a magnet too, and a compass will bring itself in line with Earth's magnetic field, so the compass always points north.*

*In this lesson, we are going to learn more about what magnets are, what a magnetic field is, and all kinds of things that use magnets. Then we will research to learn more about how magnets are used in our world. To begin, let's fill in a Main Idea and Details Sheet. We will use this worksheet to take notes about details as we read the PebbleGo article. Taking notes is a helpful way to keep track of what we learn. We can use our notes later when we do a little more research on where magnets are found.*

*Let's write the main idea in the first box of the sheet. We are going to write the word Magnets. That is the main idea of this article, or what the article is about. Today we are going to read the PebbleGo article "Magnetism." As we read, let's fill in the details about magnets.*

Depending on the level of support needed, have students read or listen to the article, or read the article to students. The instruction that follows will help to support comprehension of the content as well as connect students to the science topic.

# Vocabulary support

Be on the lookout for vocabulary words that students do not know. Encourage students to share these words with the class. Students can use strategies, such as searching for examples of the unknown word, in order to understand the word's meaning.

*I noticed some of you were not sure what the word "iron" means. (From Magnetic Field) Let's take a closer look at the sentence it is in to see if there is a clue, or hint, to its meaning. The sentence says, "All magnets attract objects made of iron." We know from this sentence that iron is an object, but lots of things are objects. I wonder if we can find other hints to its meaning by reading on. The section continues with, "Nails and paper clips stick to magnets." We already know that magnets attract objects made of iron. This next sentence gives a few examples of these objects, like nails and paper clips. I think nails and paper clips are examples of iron. I know nails and paper clips are made of metal, so I think iron is kind of metal. Seeking out examples of words we don't know helps us understand unknown words.*

Have students take notes on other words that cause confusion. Explain that by clicking on the words in red, students can get a quick definition.

# Comprehension support

⇨ *What are some details we learned about magnets in the section called What Is a Magnet?* (Students may say magnets are made from metals, and some metals are found in the earth.) *Let's add these details to our worksheet.*

⇨ *Where are magnets the strongest?* (at their poles)

⇨ *What did we learn about magnets from reading this article? What kinds of things use magnets? Can we add information to our Main Idea and Details Sheet?* (Acknowledge and accept student responses. Students will likely say magnets are used to keep doors closed and for some trains.)

# Collaborative practice ✎

Have students work in groups to reread the article and come up with their own inquiry project for further research. Encourage students to think of where magnets can be found. If students need help, point to the Main Idea and Details Sheet, and review where magnets might be found. Students can use the resources listed in **Further research** or other library resources to research where magnets are found. Consider having students share what they've learned with the class.

For further study on the topic, try the activity as a class. Click on the paper and crayon icon in the "Magnetism" article, find Activity, and click on Print.

## Differentiation

For the **Collaborative practice**, encourage higher-level students to write about their topic. For learners who might require more support, it may be helpful to first bring in magnets and objects that magnets can pick up, so students can build their background knowledge. Then brainstorm where magnets can be found. It may be helpful to have a few ideas at the ready (e.g., Maglev trains, at a junkyard, school whiteboards, and so on). Be sure to use academic vocabulary during discussion.

## Further research

- Dunne, Abbie. *Magnetism.* Physical Science. North Mankato, Minn.: Capstone Press, 2017.

- James, Emily. *The Simple Science of Magnets.* Simply Science. North Mankato, Minn.: Capstone Press, 2018.

- Royston, Angela. *All About Magnetism.* All About Science. Chicago: Heinemann Library, 2016.

# Why do we need to know the weather?

## Introduce the topic

Make a connection to an experience you had with weather and how knowing about the weather helped you. A story is provided as an example, but feel free to adjust it so it relates to your own experience.

*One summer I visited my sister in Chicago. I looked at a weather forecast on the Internet, so I knew what to pack. The weather forecast matched what actually happened. The first night I was there, it rained a lot. We brought our umbrellas and wore rain boots on our walk to dinner. The next day, it didn't rain at all. It was warm and sunny, so I wore a sundress. I'm so glad I looked at the weather forecast before my trip because I had packed the right clothes for the visit.*

*Why do you think we need to know the weather? How is it helpful? (Allow time for student responses.)*

*I heard some of you say it's helpful to know the weather so you know what to wear. That is true. But there are other reasons why it's helpful to know about the weather. I like to garden, and if I know that it is going to rain later in the day, I won't water my plants. Sometimes people need to know the weather so they can plan ahead. It's also helpful to know the weather so that we're safe. For example, if a thunderstorm is coming, we know to stay inside. Or if it will be very hot, we know to bring water for a walk outside.*

*In this lesson, we are going to learn more about weather. Then we will come up with an experiment to do with weather so we know how it affects us. To begin, let's fill in a Three Column Chart. We will use this worksheet to take notes about weather as we read the PebbleGo article. Taking notes is a helpful way to keep track of what we learn. We can use our notes later when we do an experiment on weather.*

*Let's write a title for the first column. We are going to write the title Type of Weather. For the second column, we are going to write What Happens. In the third column, we will write How to Plan. As we read today, let's fill in the chart.*

Depending on the level of support needed, have students read or listen to the article, or read the article to students. The instruction that follows will help to support comprehension of the content as well as connect students to the science topic.

# Vocabulary support

Be on the lookout for vocabulary words that students do not know. Encourage students to share these words with the class. Many of the lessons in this book talk about supporting students with one strategy. Sometimes, however, there can be a tricky sentence construction with lots of academic vocabulary words that could cause confusion. This lesson includes a model for using multiple strategies.

*I struggled reading this sentence as I was reading What Is It?: "Air temperature, wind, precipitation, clouds, and sunshine all make up the weather." This sentence starts off in a way that I am not used to. It starts with a list. By reading on, I learn that this is a list of weather. I had to read and reread this sentence to better understand what it was about, and then I could look more closely at each of the words. I understood some of the words by making a connection to them. For example, when I look at a weather forecast, it usually tells me how hot or cold it is outside by degrees. That is the temperature. Sometimes I have to use a few different strategies to understand some new vocabulary.*

Have students take notes on other words that cause confusion. Explain that by clicking on the words in red, students can get a quick definition.

# Comprehension support

⇨ *What kind of weather did we learn about in Temperature?* (Students may say sunny.) *Let's make an inference. We use information in the text and what we know to make an inference. What happens when it's sunny? How do we plan for it? Let's add these details to our chart.* (Acknowledge and accept student responses.)

⇨ *What happens when there's lots of strong winds?* (It can bring rainstorms.) *Where did you find this information?* (In the section labeled Wind.)

⇨ *What did we learn about weather from reading this article? What can we add to our Three Column Chart?* (Acknowledge and accept student responses.)

# Collaborative practice ✎

Have students work in groups to reread the article and come up with an experiment on weather. Encourage students to think of experiments that might go on for a few days—such as observing forecasts and comparing them to the actual weather. If students need help, point to the Three Column Chart, and review their notes on what happens during each type of weather and how we can plan for it. Students can also use the resources listed in **Further research** or other library resources. Consider having students share what they've learned with the class.

For further study on the topic, try the activity as a class. Click on the paper and crayon icon in the "What Is Weather?" article, find Activity, and click on Print.

## Differentiation

For the **Collaborative practice**, encourage higher-level students to research the types of tools that are used when studying weather. For learners who might require more support, it may be helpful to review the academic vocabulary in the article. Have students practice using the vocabulary by writing sentences with each term. Have students dictate sentences to you as needed.

## Further research

- PebbleGo "Fall Weather"
- PebbleGo "Spring Weather"
- PebbleGo "Summer Weather"
- PebbleGo "Winter Weather"
- Rustad, Martha E. H. What Is the Weather Today? Series. North Mankato, Minn.: Capstone Press, 2017.

# What are seasons?

## Introduce the topic

*There are four seasons in the year. Who can tell me what the seasons are?* (Wait a few moments for students to respond.) *I heard some of you say that the seasons are winter, spring, summer, and fall.*

*What are some activities you like to do during the summer?* (Acknowledge and accept student responses.) *Can you do these activities during the winter? Why or why not?*

*Long ago, people had to know when each season was happening in order to stay alive. They needed to know when to plant food, when to harvest, and when to prepare for winter. In this activity, we are going to get a better understanding of seasons and why they happen. Then we are going to interview each other, so we learn what people like to do during the seasons. To begin, let's fill in a KWL chart. We will use this chart to take notes about seasons as we read the PebbleGo article "What Are Seasons?" Taking notes is a helpful way to keep track of what we learn. We can use our notes later when we're working on the questions for our interviews.*

*What do we already know about seasons? Let's write what we know in the first column.* (Model for students, such as warm weather during the summer.) *What do we want to know about seasons? Let's write what we want to know in the second column.* (Model for students, such as asking why we have warm weather during the summer. Then take some time to write student responses in the second column.)

*Today we are going to read the PebbleGo article "What Are Seasons?" As we read, let's fill in the chart with what we've learned.*

Depending on the level of support needed, have students read or listen to the article, or read the article to students. The instruction that follows will help to support comprehension of the content as well as connect students to the science topic.

# Vocabulary support

Be on the lookout for vocabulary words that students do not know. Encourage students to share these words with the class. Students can use strategies, such as looking at the pictures, in order to understand the word's meaning.

*I noticed some of you are not sure what the word "tilted" means. (From Why Are They Different?) Let's take a closer look at the sentence it is in to see if there is a clue, or hint, to its meaning. The sentence says, "The Earth is tilted." I'm not sure what the meaning of this word is just by looking at the sentence. I will try reading on. The text says, "As it orbits the sun, parts of Earth get different amounts of sunlight." I don't have a good understanding of the word just yet, so I am going to look at the picture. I see a picture of Earth, but it doesn't show Earth as I have seen it in the past. Part of Earth is leaning toward the sun. I think that is a clue to what "tilted" means. When I click on the word, I see that "to lean" is part of the definition. Looking at the picture helped me figure out the meaning of the word.*

Have students take notes on other words that cause confusion. Explain that by clicking on the words in red, students can get a quick definition.

# Comprehension support

↪ *What did we learn about in the section Why Are They Different?* (Students may say the part of Earth tilted to the sun in the summer gets more sunlight.) *Let's add these details to our chart.*

↪ *Are seasons the same everywhere? Why or why not?* (Students may say that seasons aren't the same everywhere. Encourage students to make connections to their own experiences with seasons.)

↪ *What did we learn about seasons from reading this article? What kinds of things can we add to our KWL Chart?* (Acknowledge and accept student responses.)

# Collaborative practice ✐

Have students work in groups to reread the article and to come up with questions to ask each other on what they do during the seasons. Encourage students to come up with three questions that they can ask each other. If students need help, point to the KWL Chart, and review their notes on what happens during the seasons. Students can also use the resources listed in **Further research** or other library resources. Consider having students share what they've learned with the class.

For further study on the topic, try the activity as a class. Click on the paper and crayon icon in the "What Are Seasons?" article, find Activity, and click on Print.

## Differentiation

For the **Collaborative practice**, encourage higher-level students to research how the activities that happen during the seasons in one location might be different from another location. For learners who might require more support, it might be helpful to have them collaborate with students of similar ability to ask you questions.

## Further research

• PebbleGo includes a variety of articles about the seasons. Search for Fall, Winter, Spring, and Summer for these articles.

• Schuette, Sarah L. Investigate the Seasons Series. North Mankato, Minn.: Capstone Press, 2018.

# How can we help Earth?

## Introduce the topic

Begin this session by playing the article's accompanying videos for students. Click on the Video icon in the Media toolbar, and play the two videos.

*What did these two videos show?* (Acknowledge and accept student responses.) *I heard you say that one showed Earth from space and the other showed fish swimming in the sea. These videos show us that Earth is a planet where living things can be. Today we are going to be reading about Earth and thinking of ways that it supports life. We are going to be making inferences as we read.*

*Using information in the text to figure out something is called inferring. When I read the text, I think about the clues in the text and my own experiences to make an inference. Sometimes that is called reading between the lines.*

*Today we are going to read the PebbleGo article "What Is Earth?" We are going to use a Making Inferences Chart to take notes as we read. I will ask you questions as we read. In the first column, you will write down clues from the text. In the second column, you will write down what you already know about the topic. Then you'll use both pieces of information to make an inference.*

Depending on the level of support needed, have students read or listen to the article, or read the article to students. The instruction that follows will help to support comprehension of the content as well as connect students to the science topic.

## Vocabulary support

Be on the lookout for vocabulary words that students do not know. Encourage students to share these words with the class. Students can use strategies, such as seeking out other references, in order to understand new vocabulary.

*I noticed some of you were not sure what the word "atmosphere" means.* (From One of Eight) *Let's take a closer look at the sentence it is in to see if there is a clue, or hint, to its meaning. The sentence says, "Earth's temperature, water, and atmosphere make it a good place for plants and animals to live." After reading this sentence, I understand that Earth's atmosphere helps make it a good place to live, but I'm still not sure what the meaning of the word is. Sometimes if we come across an unknown word, it's helpful to seek out another reference, like a glossary.*

*When I click on the word, I see that it means "the mixture of gases that surrounds a planet." By looking up the word in a dictionary, I learn that atmosphere is a layer of gases that surrounds a planet. Looking up the definition of atmosphere helped me understand the word better.*

Have students take notes on other words that cause confusion. Explain that by clicking on the words in red, students can get a quick definition.

## Comprehension support

⇨ *Let's look at the section called One of Eight. Why is water important? Let's fill out the Making Inferences Chart. What is in the text? Let's fill that in the first column.* (Water makes it a good place for plants and animals to live.) *What do we know about water? Let's add that to the second column.* (We need to drink water to survive.) *What inference can you make about why water is important?* (Plants and animals would not be able to live without water.)

⇨ *Let's look at the section titled Earth's Water. Is there anything we could add to our chart about water?* (Clues in the Text: Millions of animals and plants live in these waters. What I Know: Answers will vary. Inference: Water is important for living things to survive.)

⇨ *What did we learn about Earth's air? Is there an inference we can make about Earth's air?* (Acknowledge and accept student responses.)

## Collaborative practice ✎

Have students work in groups to reread the article and to come up with a tool to help Earth. For example, planting more trees could help animals and the air. Creating a tool that cleans water can make sure we protect water sources. Encourage students to think about how to protect the air, water, or habitats on Earth. If students need help, point to the Making Inferences Chart, and review their notes on the inferences they made as they read. Students can also use the resources listed in **Further research** or other library resources. Consider having students share what they've learned with the class.

For further study on the topic, try the activity as a class. Click on the paper and crayon icon in the "What Is Earth?" article, find Activity, and click on Print.

**Differentiation**

For the **Collaborative practice**, encourage higher-level students to create a poster that advertises their tool and explains why it is helpful. For learners who might require more support, it may be helpful to help them focus on just one of Earth's natural resources and discuss its importance. Help students better understand that resource by discussing how they use it in their lives. Encourage discussion and use academic vocabulary words.

**Further research**

• PebbleGo "Water"

• PebbleGo "What Is the Sky?"

• PebbleGo "Cleaning Up Litter"

## Standards

**NGSS:**
2-PS1-1

**College and Career Readiness Standards:**
CCSS.ELA-Literacy.CCRA.R.1,
CCSS.ELA-Literacy.CCRA.R.2,
CCSS.ELA-Literacy.CCRA.R.4,
CCSS.ELA-Literacy.CCRA.R.5,
CCSS.ELA-Literacy.CCRA.L.4,
CCSS.ELA-Literacy.CCRA.L.6

**AASL Standards Framework for Learners:**
I.A.1, I.B.1, I.D.2, I.D.3, III.D.1, V.C.2, VI.A.1

## Materials

- "Temperature" PebbleGo article
- Cause and Effect Chain, p. 123

## Introduce the topic

*When you go outside on a hot day, you feel heat. The sun gives us this heat. Now imagine a cup of hot chocolate. Can you picture the steam that is coming from the cup? What do you think it feels like to hold the cup? (Acknowledge and accept student responses.)*

*The cup is giving off heat. Heat is a kind of energy that makes things hot or warm. What other things give off heat energy? (Acknowledge and accept student responses.)*

*I heard some of you say that hot water can give off heat energy. So can the clothes dryer and a fire. Today we are going to read the PebbleGo article "Temperature." We are going to use a Cause and Effect Chain to take notes as we read. A cause makes something happen. For example, I kicked a ball. My kick is the cause. The ball rolling down the street is the effect. Let's practice identifying some causes and effects. What is the effect of an alarm clock buzzing? (waking up) What is the cause of someone doing really well on a quiz? (studying)*

*After we read, we are going to use our Cause and Effect Chains to come up with an experiment on heat.*

Depending on the level of support needed, have students read or listen to the article, or read the article to students. The instruction that follows will help to support comprehension of the content as well as connect students to the science topic.

## Vocabulary support

Be on the lookout for vocabulary words that students do not know. Encourage students to share these words with the class. The following is a model on context clues and can be completed with any of the terms.

*Some of you had asked me what "estimate" means. (From How It Feels) Let's take a closer look at the sentence it is in to see if there is a clue, or hint, to its meaning. The sentence says, "You can estimate temperature by how a material feels." Are there some clues that will help us figure out the word "estimate"? The author is saying we can use how something feels to estimate temperature. It sounds like we don't need a tool to know the temperature, and we can just go by how something feels. I think "estimate" means using information we already have to figure out something or make a guess about it. By clicking on the word, I learned that this definition is correct.*

Have students take notes on other words that cause confusion. Explain that by clicking on the words in red, students can get a quick definition.

# Comprehension support

↪ *Let's look at the section titled What Is a Property? What causes heat? Let's fill that in the first box under Cause.* (the movement of molecules) *Let's write the effect* (heat) *in the box under Effect.*

↪ *What happens to a thermometer when it gets warm outside?* (The liquid warms, expands, and moves upward.) *Let's fill in our chain with this cause and effect.*

↪ *What happens to water when it freezes outside? Let's fill in our chain.* (Cause: freezing weather; Effect: water freezes) *Where did we see this information?* (Celsius and Fahrenheit)

↪ *What did we learn about temperature? Are there additional items we can add to our Cause and Effect Chain?* (Acknowledge and accept student responses. Provide an additional copy of the worksheet or have students write on the back of it if they have additional causes and effects.)

# Collaborative practice ✎

Have students work in groups to reread the article and to come up with an experiment they can try to create heat. For example, they can rub two hands together or rub an eraser against a piece of paper. Encourage students to think of the steps needed to create heat. They may need to be reminded of the definition of heat in order to work on this activity. If students need help, point to the Cause and Effect Chain to review their notes. Students can also use the resources listed in **Further research** or other library resources. Consider having students share what they've learned with the class.

For further study on the topic, try the activity as a class. Click on the paper and crayon icon in the "Temperature" article, find Activity, and click on Print.

## Differentiation

For the **Collaborative practice**, encourage higher-level students to provide an explanation of how heat was created. For learners who might require more support, it may be helpful to model an experiment for students prior to having them try the activity on their own. Use academic vocabulary during the discussion.

## Further research

- PebbleGo "Hot or Cold?"
- PebbleGo "Energy"
- Thomas, Isabel. *Experiments with Heating and Cooling.* Read and Experiment. Chicago: Heinemann Library, 2015.

## Where does light come from?

**Standards**

**NGSS:**
K-PS3-1, K-PS3-2, 1-PS4-2,
2-PS1-1, K-2-ETS1-1

**College and Career
Readiness Standards:**
CCSS.ELA-Literacy.CCRA.R.1,
CCSS.ELA-Literacy.CCRA.R.2,
CCSS.ELA-Literacy.CCRA.R.4,
CCSS.ELA-Literacy.CCRA.L.4,
CCSS.ELA-Literacy.CCRA.L.5,
CCSS.ELA-Literacy.CCRA.L.6

**AASL Standards
Framework for Learners:**
I.A.2, I.B.1, I.D.3, III.D.1, VI.A.1

**Materials**

- "What Is Light?" PebbleGo
  article
- KWL Chart, p. 116

### Introduce the topic

*Look all around the classroom. What are some things that you can see?*
(Acknowledge and accept student responses.)

*I heard some of you say that you could see my desk, student desks, posters, and
books. There are lots of things we can see in the room. How do you think we're able
to see all of these items?* (Acknowledge and accept student responses.)

*That's right! There's a light overhead, so we can see these things around us.*
(Depending on whether your classroom has a window, you could also
mention that the window streams in light from the sun.)

*Today we are going to learn about where light comes from. To begin, let's fill in a
KWL Chart. We will use this chart to take notes about light as we read the PebbleGo
article. Taking notes is a helpful way to keep track of what we learn. We can use our
notes later when we're working on a project about properties of light.*

*What do we already know about light? Let's write what we know in the first
column.* (Model for students, such as light comes from the sun.) *What do we
want to know about light? Let's write what we want to know in the second column.*
(Model for students, such as asking if light is always hot. Then take some
time to write student responses in the second column.)

*Today we are going to read the PebbleGo article "What Is Light?" As we read, let's
fill in the chart with information that we learned.*

Depending on the level of support needed, have students read or listen to
the article, or read the article to students. The instruction that follows will
help to support comprehension of the content as well as connect students to
the science topic.

# Vocabulary support

Be on the lookout for vocabulary words that students do not know. Encourage students to share these words with the class. The following is a model on word relationships and can be completed with some of the terms.

*Some of you were not sure what "translucent" means. (From Transparent or Translucent?) We could take a closer look at the sentence to see if there is a clue, or hint, to its meaning. The sentence says, "Translucent things scatter some light." I'm not quite sure what the word means from the sentence, so I am going to read on. The text says things look blurry through something translucent, but I'm still not sure what the word means. I noticed the text talked about how things that are transparent let the light through, like a window. It seems things that are translucent aren't very clear. I could better understand translucent by pairing it up with transparent. Translucent seems to let some light through but not enough. Looking at how words are related helped me understand an unknown word.*

Have students take notes on other words that cause confusion. Explain that by clicking on the words in red, students can get a quick definition.

# Comprehension support

⇨ *Let's look at the section titled What Is Light? It says that light travels in a ray. How is it that we're able to see things?* (Light bounces off from the things to our eyes.) *This helps explain what light is. Was this information new to you? If so, add it to the What I Learned column in the KWL chart.*

⇨ *Light comes from lots of sources. Were any of these sources new to you? Add them to the chart. What do you think some of the properties, or features, are of those light sources?* (Properties could be color, temperature, and so on.)

⇨ *What kinds of objects don't let in a lot of light? Where did you find this information?* (objects that are translucent or opaque; Transparent or Translucent? Blocking or Reflecting?)

# Collaborative practice ✐

Have students work in groups to reread the article and to think about all of the places where light could come from. Encourage students to list these sources and write the properties of each. If students need help, point to the KWL Chart to review their notes. Students can also use the resources listed in **Further research** or other library resources. For more information on properties, students can read or listen to the PebbleGo article "Hot or Cold?" Consider having students share what they've learned with the class.

For further study on the topic, try the activity as a class. Click on the paper and crayon icon in the "What Is Light?" article, find Activity, and click on Print.

## Differentiation

For the **Collaborative practice**, encourage higher-level students to think of a tool they can design that could help people be outside during a sunny day. For learners who might require more support, it may be helpful to break things down by discussing sources of light that are really hot, like fire or the sunlight. From there, students can compare a hot source of light to a source that is not hot, such as a TV.

## Further research

- PebbleGo "Colors"
- PebbleGo "Sunlight"
- James, Emily. *The Simple Science of Light.* Simply Science. North Mankato, Minn.: Capstone Press, 2018.

# What is sound?

## Toolbars

There is a toolbar of related resources that can be printed (Print toolbar) and another that can be viewed (Media toolbar).

### Print

› Cite icon (pencil and paper): Students may need to reference the article should they be writing a report. They can click on this icon to see the citation as well as highlight it, copy it, and paste it into their report. The citation can also be printed out, placed at learning centers, and used as a reference.

› Article icon (papers): If you'd like to have a printout of the article or the images for center work, click on this icon. Either or both can be printed out.

› Activities icon (crayon and paper): The "Sound" article includes a Share what you know activity. You can print this out for students to work on. Consider placing it at a center, and encourage students to work collaboratively on the activity. Other activities include a Physical Sciences: What Is Sound? activity, which is an experiment on sound, and a Questions for Understanding worksheet.

### Media

› Video icon (TV): Before or after reading the article, encourage students to watch the videos for more information about sound. There are two videos in this section.

Each PebbleGo article has many resources that will help encourage learning about the topic. This lesson explores the resources that appear in the "Sound" article. Encourage students to review these assets in order to answer the question, "What is sound?" The format of this lesson may be used to introduce most PebbleGo articles. Some articles may have different asset types.

## Article features

Articles have a number of features that you will want to go over with students.

➪ Each article provides content by tabs, with each tab on one main idea. With "Sound," there is a tab on What Is Sound?, Sound and Matter, Sound Waves Travel, Pitch, and How We Hear Sound. An activity on exploring main idea and details would be a perfect way to introduce the tabs to students.

➪ Students can read the article or have it read to them by clicking on the speaker icon.

➪ Academic terms are highlighted in red. By clicking on the word and the speaker icon, students can read and hear a glossary definition of the word.

➪ Each tab includes a picture that supports the text.

➪ The related articles for "Sound" can be seen by doing a search on Physical Sciences. These articles include "Light" and "Matter."

### Standards

**NGSS:**
1-PS4-1, 2-PS1-1

**College and Career Readiness Standards:**
CCSS.ELA-Literacy.CCRA.R.7, CCSS.ELA-Literacy.CCRA.R.9

**AASL Standards Framework for Learners:**
I.A.2, I.D.3, VI.A.1

### Materials

• "Sound" PebbleGo article

# How are day and night different around the world?

## Standards

**NGSS:**
K-PS3-1, 1-ESS1-1

**College and Career Readiness Standards:**
CCSS.ELA-Literacy.CCRA.R.1,
CCSS.ELA-Literacy.CCRA.R.2,
CCSS.ELA-Literacy.CCRA.R.4,
CCSS.ELA-Literacy.CCRA.L.4,
CCSS.ELA-Literacy.CCRA.L.6

**AASL Standards Framework for Learners:**
I.A.1, I.A.2, I.D.2, I.D.3, III.D.1, VI.A.1

## Materials

- "Day and Night" PebbleGo article
- Question Words Chart, p. 119
- Map of the world
- Time zone converter (can be found online)

## Introduce the topic

*What do we see during the day?* (Allow some time for students to respond.) *That's right, we see the Sun! And during the night, we see the Moon. Day begins with the Sun, and night begins with the Moon.*

*What are some activities you like to do during the day? What do you do at night?* (Acknowledge and accept student responses.)

*Today we are going to learn more about what makes day happen and what makes night happen. To begin, let's fill in a Question Words Chart.* (Review question words as needed.) *We will use this chart to write down our questions about day and night before, during, and after we read the PebbleGo article "Day and Night." We will also add answers as we read. Taking notes is a helpful way to keep track of what we learn.*

*What are some questions we have about day and night? For example, what happens during the day? What about at night? Let's write these questions on the chart and then fill in the chart with our answers.* (Model for students, such as going to school and going to bed.) *What are some other questions we have about day and night? Where might we get the answers to these questions?* (Acknowledge student responses, filling in the correct part of the chart.)

*Today we are going to read the PebbleGo article "Day and Night." As we read, let's fill in the chart with some new questions we have and the answers, if they appear in the article.*

Depending on the level of support needed, have students read or listen to the article, or read the article to students. The instruction that follows will help to support comprehension of the content as well as connect students to the science topic.

**Science Lessons:** How are day and night different around the world?

37

# Vocabulary support

Be on the lookout for vocabulary words that students do not know. Encourage students to share these words with the class. Students can use strategies, such as using context clues, in order to understand the word's meaning.

*I noticed some of you were not sure what the word "rotation" means.* (From How It Happens) *Let's take a closer look at the sentence it is in to see if there is a clue, or hint, to its meaning. The sentence says, "One rotation takes one day, or 24 hours." I'm not sure what the meaning of this word is just by looking at the sentence. I will try reading on. The text says, "As it spins, part of Earth faces the sun." I think the word "spins" is related to "rotation." It is a clue to what "rotation" means. When I click on the word, I see that "one complete spin" is part of the definition. Reading on and looking at the glossary helped me figure out the meaning of an unknown word.*

Have students take notes on other words that cause confusion. Explain that by clicking on the words in red, students can get a quick definition.

# Comprehension support

➪ *What did we learn about the section called What Are They?* (Students may say day and night are opposites.) *Let's add the question and these details to our chart.*

➪ *Does everyone have day and night at the same time? Why or why not?* (Students may say that when we have day, other places don't because that part of Earth faces away from the sun.)

➪ *What did we learn about day and night from reading this article? What kinds of questions and answers can we add to our Question Words Chart? Were there questions you had that were not answered in the article?* (Acknowledge and accept student responses.)

# Collaborative practice ✎

Have students work in groups to reread the article and to come up with five different times and the things they do during those times. The times should be a mix of day and night activities. Have them write down their ideas. Then have students select three countries. They can look at the globe for help. Work with students to convert the times they chose to the times in those other countries. Then students can determine whether these other countries might experience the same activities at the same time. Students can also use the resources listed in **Further research** or other library resources. Consider having students share what they've learned with the class.

For further study on the topic, try the activity as a class. Click on the paper and crayon icon in the "Day and Night" article, find Activity, and click on Print.

# What's in the night's sky?

## Introduce the topic

*Think about the sky at night. What are some things we can see?* (Acknowledge and accept student responses.)

*I heard some of you say the Moon, the stars, and possibly a planet. What are some things you wonder about the night's sky?* (Model for students. For example, perhaps you wonder what the Moon is made of.)

*Today we are going to learn more about one item in our night's sky, the Moon. To begin, let's fill in a KWL Chart about the Moon. What do we already know about the Moon? Let's write what we know in the first column.* (Model for students, such as we often see the Moon at night.) *What do we want to know about the Moon? Let's write what we want to know in the second column.* (Model for students, such as asking what the Moon is made of. Then take some time to write student responses in the second column.)

*Today we are going to read the PebbleGo article "The Moon." As we read, let's fill in the chart. We will fill in the last column with information that we learned. We will use this information to come up with some wonderings we have about the night's sky and then do further research on something we wonder about.*

Depending on the level of support needed, have students read or listen to the article, or read the article to students. The instruction that follows will help to support comprehension of the content as well as connect students to the science topic.

## Vocabulary support

Be on the lookout for vocabulary words that students do not know. Encourage students to share these words with the class. Students can use strategies, such as using picture support, in order to understand the word's meaning.

*I noticed some of you were not sure what the word "layer" means.* (From What Is It Made Of?) *Let's take a closer look at the sentence it is in to see if there is a clue, or hint, to its meaning. The sentence says, "The top layer of the Moon is the crust." I now know the layer is at the top and it's called the crust, but I'm still not sure what it means. I could look at the picture to help me understand. There is a layer shown at the top part of the Moon.*

## Standards

**NGSS:**
1-ESS1-1

**College and Career Readiness Standards:**
CCSS.ELA-Literacy.CCRA.R.1,
CCSS.ELA-Literacy.CCRA.R.2,
CCSS.ELA-Literacy.CCRA.R.4,
CCSS.ELA-Literacy.CCRA.L.6,
CCSS.ELA-Literacy.CCRA.L.7

**AASL Standards Framework for Learners:**
I.A.1, I.A.2, I.B.2, I.B.3, I.D.2, III.D.1, IV.B.1, V.C.1, VI.A.1

## Materials

- "The Moon" PebbleGo article
- KWL Chart, p. 116
- Art supplies: construction paper, markers, and crayons

*When I click on the word, I see that it means "a thickness or coating of something," and the picture does show the layer as something that is coating the Moon. Looking at the picture and reading its definition helped me figure out the meaning of an unknown word.*

Have students take notes on other words that cause confusion. Explain that by clicking on the words in red, students can get a quick definition.

# Comprehension support

⤷ *What did we learn about the Moon from reading the section called What Is It?* (Students may say the Moon is a satellite and is much smaller than Earth.) *Let's add these details to our chart.*

⤷ *My wondering about what the Moon is made of is answered in this article. What does the article say? Where did we find this information?* (Students may say the Moon is made of rock and iron, and the information was found in What Is It Made Of?)

⤷ *What did we learn about the Moon by reading this article? What can we add to our KWL Chart?* (Acknowledge and accept student responses.)

# Collaborative practice ✎

Have students continue making wonderings about the night's sky. This project should not be limited to just the Moon. Encourage student pairs to do further research about their wondering. Then they could use art supplies to draw and color the item they researched. Encourage students to add labels or captions to help explain their wondering. Students can use the resources listed in **Further research** or other library resources. Consider having students share what they've learned with the class.

For further study on the topic, try the activity as a class. Click on the paper and crayon icon in "The Moon" article, find Activity, and click on Print.

# What is the difference between living things and nonliving things?

## Introduce the topic

*Today we are going to talk about living and nonliving things. What is one example of a living thing?* (Acknowledge and accept student responses.)

*I heard some of you say your pet dog is a living thing. The trees outside are living things too. What do living things have in common?* (Students will likely say that living things need food and water.) *What is an example of a nonliving thing?* (Acknowledge and accept student responses.)

*I heard some of you say that rocks are nonliving things. What do you know about nonliving things?* (Acknowledge and accept student responses.)

*I heard some of you say that nonliving things were never alive. They don't need food or water or air.*

*In this lesson, we are going to learn more about living and nonliving things. Then we will use what we learn to make a checklist about living things. To begin, let's start a Venn diagram. We are going to write Nonliving Things as the title for the first circle. We are going to write the title Living Things in the second circle. We are going to title the place where the two sections meet as Both. We are going to fill in the Venn diagram as we read the PebbleGo article. Taking notes is a helpful way to keep track of what we know and learn. We can use our notes later when we create our checklist of features, or traits, of living things.*

*Today we are going to read the PebbleGo article "Living or Nonliving." As we read, let's fill in the Venn diagram with what we learned. If we see a trait for a nonliving thing, we'll add it to the first circle. If we see a trait for a living thing, we'll add it to the second circle. If both nonliving and living things have a trait, we'll write it in the place where the two circles meet.*

### Standards

NGSS:
K-LS1-1

**College and Career Readiness Standards:**
CCSS.ELA-Literacy.CCRA.R.1,
CCSS.ELA-Literacy.CCRA.R.2,
CCSS.ELA-Literacy.CCRA.R.4,
CCSS.ELA-Literacy.CCRA.L.4,
CCSS.ELA-Literacy.CCRA.L.5,
CCSS.ELA-Literacy.CCRA.L.6

**AASL Standards Framework for Learners:**
I.A.2, I.B.1, I.D.2, I.D.3, III.A.2, III.D.1, IV.B.1, VI.A.1

### Materials

- "Living or Nonliving" PebbleGo article
- Venn Diagram, p. 122

**Science Lessons:** What is the difference between living things and nonliving things?

41

Depending on the level of support needed, have students read or listen to the article, or read the article to students. The instruction that follows will help to support comprehension of the content as well as connect students to the science topic.

# Vocabulary support

Be on the lookout for vocabulary words that students do not know. Encourage students to share these words with the class. Students can use strategies, such as searching for examples that describe an unknown word, in order to understand the word's meaning.

*I noticed some of you were not sure what the word "react" means. (From Move and React) Let's take a closer look at the sentence it is in to see if there is a clue, or hint, to its meaning. The sentence says, "They also react to things around them." We don't know what the word means from that sentence, so let's read on for clues. The next two sentences say, "Plants bend toward sunlight. Dogs chase balls." These must be examples of how living things react. Based on these examples, I know to react is to respond to something. By clicking on the word I see the definition for "react" is to respond. Sometimes it's helpful to read on to see whether there are examples of an unknown word.*

Have students take notes on other words that cause confusion. Explain that by clicking on the words in red, students can get a quick definition.

# Comprehension support

⤷ *What did we learn about nonliving and living things in the section titled Living and Nonliving?* (Frogs and water lilies are living things. Water and rocks are nonliving things.)

⤷ *What do living things need? Which section did we read this in? Is there anything we can add to our Venn diagram?* (Acknowledge and accept student responses. Living things need energy, food, air, and water; found in Food, Air, and Water; can add need energy, food, air, and water to Venn diagram.)

⤷ *What did we learn about living and nonliving things from reading this article? Can we add information to our Venn diagram?* (Acknowledge and accept student responses.)

# Collaborative practice ✐

Have students work in groups to come up with a checklist of the features of living things. Students can refer to the living things included in the article as well as other living things they can think of. Students can use the resources listed in **Further research** or other library resources. Consider having students share what they've learned with the class.

For further study on the topic, try the activity as a class. Click on the paper and crayon icon in the "Living and Nonliving" article, find Activity, and click on Print.

## Differentiation

For the **Collaborative practice**, encourage higher-level students to come up another checklist for nonliving things. For learners who might require more support, it may be helpful to provide them with pictures of things that are alive and to talk as a small group about what these things have in common.

## Further research

- PebbleGo "What Are Plants?"
- PebbleGo "What Are Animals?"
- PebbleGo "What Are Humans?"
- Rissman, Rebecca. Is It Living or Nonliving? Series. North Mankato, Minn.: Capstone Press, 2014.

*A Year of PebbleGo®: Connecting Content to Literacy*

# How are young like their parents?

Each PebbleGo article has many resources that will help encourage learning about the topic. This lesson explores the resources that appear in the "Heredity" article. Encourage students to review these assets in order to answer the question, "How are young like their parents?" The format of this lesson may be used to introduce most PebbleGo articles. Some articles may have different asset types.

## Article features

Articles have a number of features that you will want to go over with students.

⇨ Each article provides content by tabs, with each tab on one main idea. With "Heredity," there is a tab on Offspring, Like Parents, Variations, Advantages, and Environment. An activity on exploring main idea and details would be a perfect way to introduce the tabs to students.

⇨ Students can read the article or have it read to them by clicking on the speaker icon.

⇨ Academic terms are highlighted in red. By clicking on the word and the speaker icon, students can read and hear a glossary definition of the word.

⇨ Each tab includes a picture that supports the text.

⇨ The related articles for "Heredity" can be seen by doing a search on Life Sciences. There are a variety of plants and animals articles from which to choose. There are also articles on "Humans," "Living or Nonliving," "Cells," and "Adaptations."

## Standards

**NGSS:**
1-LS1-2, 1-LS3-1

**College and Career Readiness Standards:**
CCSS.ELA-Literacy.CCRA.R.7, CCSS.ELA-Literacy.CCRA.R.9

**AASL Standards Framework for Learners:**
I.A.2, I.D.3, VI.A.1

## Materials

• "Heredity" PebbleGo article

## Toolbars

There is a toolbar of related resources that can be printed (Print toolbar) and another that can be viewed (Media toolbar).

### Print

> Cite icon (pencil and paper): Students may need to reference the article should they be writing a report. They can click on this icon to see the citation as well as highlight it, copy it, and paste it into their report. The citation can also be printed out, placed at learning centers, and used as a reference.

> Article icon (papers): If you'd like to have a printout of the article or the images for center work, click on this icon. Either or both can be printed out.

> Activities icon (crayon and paper): The "Heredity" article includes a Share what you know activity. You can print this out for students to work on. Consider placing it at a center, and encourage students to work collaboratively on the activity. Other activities include a Life Sciences: Heredity activity, which is an activity on environment and heredity, and a Questions for Understanding worksheet.

### Media

> Video icon (TV): Before or after reading the article, encourage students to watch the videos for more information about heredity. There are two videos in this section.

## Standards

**NGSS:**
K-LS1-1, K-ESS3-1, K-2-ETS1-2

**College and Career Readiness Standards:**
CCSS.ELA-Literacy.CCRA.R.1,
CCSS.ELA-Literacy.CCRA.R.2,
CCSS.ELA-Literacy.CCRA.R.4,
CCSS.ELA-Literacy.CCRA.L.4,
CCSS.ELA-Literacy.CCRA.L.6

**AASL Standards Framework for Learners:**
I.A.1, I.A.2, I.B.1, I.D.2, III.A.2,
III.D.1, IV.B.1, VI.A.1

## Materials

- "Adaptations" PebbleGo article
- Three Column Chart, p. 115
- Art supplies: construction paper, modeling clay

# How do animals survive?

## Introduce the topic

*A basic need is something living things need to survive, or to live. We need food to survive. What are some of our other basic needs?* (Acknowledge and accept student responses.)

*I heard some of you say that we need water and air. Those are some of our basic needs. Another basic need is shelter, or the place where we live. Animals have basic needs too. Sometimes animals have adaptations so they are able to live in a certain place. This means they had to change in order to survive. For example, the feet of a camel are very large and can spread out. This adaptation helps the camel walk on sand. Some animals need to be able to blend in with their surroundings to protect them from other animals. What are some other adaptations you can think of?* (Acknowledge and accept student responses.)

*In this lesson, we are going to learn about adaptations. Then we are going to take what we learn to think of a real place an animal might live, or its habitat, and make up an animal that might live there. We'll think about the adaptations it needs to have in order to live there. We are going to start with a Three Column Chart. We will title the first column Place, the second column Animal, and the third column Adaptation. We are going to fill in the Three Column Chart as we read the PebbleGo article. Taking notes is a helpful way to keep track of what we know and learn. We can use our notes later when we make up our animal.*

*Today we are going to read the PebbleGo article "Adaptations." As we read, let's fill in the Three Column Chart with what we learned.*

Depending on the level of support needed, have students read or listen to the article, or read the article to students. The instruction that follows will help to support comprehension of the content as well as connect students to the science topic.

# Vocabulary support

Be on the lookout for vocabulary words that students do not know. Encourage students to share these words with the class. Students can use strategies, such as searching for the definition of an unknown word within the text, in order to understand the word's meaning.

*I noticed some of you are not sure what the word "habitat" means.* (From Adaptations) *Let's take a closer look at the sentence it is in to see if there is a clue, or hint, to its meaning. The sentence says, "A habitat is the place where a plant or animal lives." This sentence gives the definition of the word, so now I understand what it means. By clicking on the word, there is further explanation of it. Sometimes authors include the definition of a word right in the sentence. Why do you think they do this?* (Acknowledge and accept student responses.) *I heard a lot of different answers. One student thought the author does this to provide a definition of a tricky word in the text. Another thought the author does it to begin an article about adaptations. The author was giving us some background information right in the text. These are all good reasons why the author might include the definition of a word in the text.*

Have students take notes on other words that cause confusion. Explain that by clicking on the words in red, students can get a quick definition.

# Comprehension support

▷ *What did we learn about sharks in the Body Shape section?* (The shark's shape helps it swim in the water.) *Let's add this information to the Three Column Chart. Is there other information from this section that we can add to our charts?* (air, bird, wings; ground, gopher, strong legs)

▷ *Take a look at the Life in Deserts section. How are camels able to live in the desert?* (They have a hump to store food and water. Their feet help them walk on hot sand.) *Let's add these items to our chart.*

▷ *What did we learn about adaptations by reading this article? Can we add information to our chart?* (Acknowledge and accept student responses.)

# Collaborative practice ✐

Have students work in groups to make up an animal that can survive in a habitat. Students can refer to the living things included in the article as well as other living things they can think of. Encourage students to refer to the Three Column Chart. Students can also use the resources listed in **Further research** or other library resources. Consider having students share what they've learned with the class.

For further study on the topic, try the activity as a class. Click on the paper and crayon icon in the "Adaptations" article, find Activity, and click on Print.

## Differentiation

For the **Collaborative practice**, encourage all students to create a model of their animal. They can draw it or create a 3-D model using art supplies. Consider having students collaborate in mixed-ability groupings. For learners who might require more support, it may be helpful to provide them with pictures of different habitats and the animals that live there.

## Further research

- PebbleGo "Desert Animals"
- PebbleGo "Grassland Animals"
- PebbleGo "Ocean Animals"
- PebbleGo "Rain Forest Animals"
- PebbleGo "Wetland Animals"
- PebbleGo "Woodland Animals"
- Amstutz, Lisa J. *Kings of the Deserts*. Animal Rulers. North Mankato, Minn.: Capstone Press, 2018.

# What are plants?

## Introduce the topic

Begin this lesson by playing Video 1 in the Media toolbar. Ask students what they notice about the video.

*I heard some of you say that you saw the plant grow from seed to plant. What plant parts did you see in the video? (Students will likely say the seed, stem, and leaves.) Like all living things, plants have a life cycle. Their life cycle often starts with a seed. As it grows, its parts grow too. Unlike other living things, plants cannot move around.*

*As we read today, we will take notes. We are going to start with a T-Chart. We will label the first column Plant Part and the second column What It Does. We are going to fill in the T-Chart as we read the PebbleGo article. Taking notes is a helpful way to keep track of what we know and learn. We can use our notes later when we make our plant life cycles.*

*Today we are going to read the PebbleGo article "What Are Plants?" As we read, let's fill in the T-Chart with what we learned.*

Depending on the level of support needed, have students read or listen to the article, or read the article to students. The instruction that follows will help to support comprehension of the content as well as connect students to the science topic.

## Vocabulary support

Be on the lookout for vocabulary words that students do not know. Encourage students to share these words with the class. Students can use strategies, such as using a glossary and dictionary, in order to understand the word's meaning.

*I noticed some of you were not sure what the word "cells" means. (From What Are Plants?) Let's take a closer look at the sentence it is in to see if there is a clue, or hint, to its meaning. The sentence says, "They are made of many cells." I don't have a clear idea of what "cells" means from this sentence, so I will read on. (Take a moment to read the section to the group.) Sometimes authors include clues to the meaning of a word in the sentence or the surrounding sentences. This time, there are no clues for cells, so I will try to find its meaning in another resource, like the glossary.*

*When I click on the word, I learned more information about it. I learned that it is a tiny structure of a living thing. From looking it up in a dictionary, I learned that a cell is a small unit of a living thing. From these definitions, I understand that a cell is a small unit in a living thing. Living things must have many cells. By looking up the definition, I was able to learn a new word.*

Have students take notes on other words that cause confusion. Explain that by clicking on the words in red, students can get a quick definition.

## Comprehension support

↪ *What did we learn about plants in the section called What Plants Need?* (Plants need sunlight, air, and water to make food.)

↪ *Take a look at the section called Leaves, Stems, and Roots. Is there information we can add to our T-Chart?* (leaves, make a plant's food; roots, take in water and minerals; stems, carry food and water to the rest of the plant) *Let's add these items to our chart.*

↪ *What did we learn about plants from the part called Reproduction? Is there anything we can add to our T-Chart?* (Acknowledge and accept student responses; seeds, to reproduce.)

↪ It will be helpful for **Collaborative practice** to go over the life cycle of a plant. Revisit the video while discussing the life cycle.

## Collaborative practice ✎

Have students work in groups to draw a life cycle of a plant. Students can refer to the "What Are Plants?" article as well as the T-Chart for guidance. Students can use the resources listed in **Further research** or other library resources. Consider having students share what they've learned with the class.

For further study on the topic, try the activity as a class. Click on the paper and crayon icon in the "What Are Plants?" article, find Activity, and click on Print.

### Differentiation

For **Collaborative practice**, consider having higher-level students write about the plant's life cycle. For learners who require more support, it might be helpful to show them pictures from the life cycle of a plant and go over the steps. Then transfer that information to new images of a plant's life cycle, and have the students point out the steps.

### Further research

• PebbleGo "Flowering Plants"

• Dunn, Mary R. *An Apple Tree's Life Cycle.* Explore Life Cycles. North Mankato, Minn.: Capstone Press, 2018.

• Dunn, Mary R. *A Bean's Life Cycle.* Explore Life Cycles. North Mankato, Minn.: Capstone Press, 2018.

• Dunn, Mary R. *A Sunflower's Life Cycle.* Explore Life Cycles. North Mankato, Minn.: Capstone Press, 2018.

## Standards

**NGSS:**
K-LS1-1, 1-LS1-1

**College and Career Readiness Standards:**
CCSS.ELA-Literacy.CCRA.R.1,
CCSS.ELA-Literacy.CCRA.R.2,
CCSS.ELA-Literacy.CCRA.R.4,
CCSS.ELA-Literacy.CCRA.R.7,
CCSS.ELA-Literacy.CCRA.L.4,
CCSS.ELA-Literacy.CCRA.L.6

**AASL Standards Framework for Learners:**
I.A.1, I.A.2, I.D.1, I.D.2, I.D.3,
III.A.2, III.D.1, V.C.1, VI.A.1

## Materials

- "Flowering Plants" PebbleGo article
- Making Connections Chart, p. 118
- Art supplies: construction paper, markers, and crayons

# What are the different plant types?

## Introduce the topic

*Close your eyes and imagine you are walking in a neighborhood. What kinds of plants do you see?* (Acknowledge and accept student responses.) *There are all kinds of plants, from big trees to medium-sized bushes to colorful flowers.*

*Today we are going to make connections as we read. Some of the connections we have to a text are things we read in another text. A second kind of connection is making a connection to ourselves. Some of the topics we read about in books we may have seen or experienced firsthand. The final connection is to our world. This means we've heard about the topic in our world, such as on TV.*

*Today we are going to read the PebbleGo article "Flowering Plants." As we read, let's fill in the Making Connections Chart with what we learned. Then we are going to research different kinds of plants and continue using the chart during our research.*

Depending on the level of support needed, have students read or listen to the article, or read the article to students. The instruction that follows will help to support comprehension of the content as well as connect students to the science topic.

## Vocabulary support

Be on the lookout for vocabulary words that students do not know. Encourage students to share these words with the class. Students can use multiple strategies, such as searching for context clues and looking at affixes, in order to understand the word's meaning.

*I noticed some of you were not sure what the word "inedible" means.* (From Fruits and Seeds) *Let's take a closer look at the sentence it is in to see if there is a clue, or hint, to its meaning. The sentence says, "Other fruits are inedible." I don't have a clear idea of what "inedible" means from this sentence, so I will reread the section.* (Take a moment to read the section to the group.) *I noticed the section talks about fruit we can eat. Then it explains that some fruits are inedible.*

*I think the word "eat" is a clue to what inedible means. I also noticed "inedible" has the prefix "in." This prefix can mean "not." So "inedible" must mean something that we cannot do. "Edible" sounds like "eat," so I think "inedible" means something we cannot eat. By clicking on the word, I learn that it means "not fit to be eaten." By using different strategies, such as rereading the section to look for clues, looking at prefixes, and looking up the word, I now have a better understanding of what the word means.*

Have students take notes on other words that cause confusion. Explain that by clicking on the words in red, students can get a quick definition.

## Comprehension support

⇨ *What did we learn about flowering plants in the section called What Are Flowering Plants?* (These plants have roots, stems, leaves, flowers, and fruit.) *Is there a connection you can make to this section? Let's add it to our charts.* (Acknowledge and accept student responses.)

⇨ *Take a look at the section called Pollen. Have you ever seen a bee carry pollen? Or have you read about pollen? Let's add that information to our charts.*

⇨ *What did you learn about flowering plants from Fruits and Seeds? Add this information along with a connection you can make to the chart.*

## Collaborative practice ✎

Students have just learned about flowering plants, but there are many different kinds of plants. In this practice, students will have the opportunity to pick one type of plant, research it, and talk about it with the class. They could use a new Making Connections Chart to take notes, or take notes by freehand. Students may find the chart helpful in understanding the content a little better. Have students work in groups to select one plant to research, to draw, and to label its parts. Students can research their plant by using one of the PebbleGo articles listed in **Further research** or by using other library resources. Consider having students share what they've learned with the class.

For further study on the topic, try the activity as a class. Click on the paper and crayon icon in the "Flowering Plants" article, find Activity, and click on Print.

### Differentiation

For the **Collaborative practice**, encourage students to select one person from their group to present their plant and its parts. For learners who might require more support, have students research a plant they are most familiar with. Encourage students to think about where they may have seen the plant while out and about.

### Further research

- PebbleGo "Conifers"
- PebbleGo "Ferns"
- PebbleGo "Mosses"

# What are animals?

## Standards

**NGSS:**
K-LS1-1, K-ESS3-1, 2-LS4-1

**College and Career Readiness Standards:**
CCSS.ELA-Literacy.CCRA.R.1,
CCSS.ELA-Literacy.CCRA.R.2,
CCSS.ELA-Literacy.CCRA.R.4,
CCSS.ELA-Literacy.CCRA.R.7,
CCSS.ELA-Literacy.CCRA.W.7,
CCSS.ELA-Literacy.CCRA.L.4,
CCSS.ELA-Literacy.CCRA.L.5,
CCSS.ELA-Literacy.CCRA.L.6

**AASL Standards Framework for Learners:**
I.A.1, I.A.2, I.D.1, I.D.2, III.A.1,
III.A.2, III.D.1, V.C.1, VI.A.1

## Materials

- "What Are Animals?" PebbleGo article
- KWL Chart, p. 116

## Introduce the topic

*Today we are going to talk about animals. What are some animals you know about?* (List students' responses as they share out.)

*Where do the animals live? How do they move?* (Acknowledge and accept student responses.) *I heard one of you talk about a snake and that it lives in the desert and slithers around. The fact that it can live in a really hot place makes it pretty special. What other animals live in the desert?* (Acknowledge and accept student responses.)

*Think of an animal you want to know more about. Write the animal's name on the KWL chart. What do you already know about the animal? Write it in your chart under the column What I Know. What do you want to know about the animal? Write your wonderings in the part of the chart labeled What I Want to Know. As we read the PebbleGo article "What Are Animals?," we can add more information to our chart. You may have more questions. Add them to the What I Want to Know column. If you find the answers as you read today, add that information to What I Learned. After we read, we will do more research about the animal.*

Depending on the level of support needed, have students read or listen to the article, or read the article to students. The instruction that follows will help to support comprehension of the content as well as connect students to the science topic.

## Vocabulary support

Be on the lookout for vocabulary words that students do not know. Encourage students to share these words with the class. Students can use strategies, such as the Four-Square strategy. This strategy works well by taking a piece of paper, folding it lengthwise, and then folding it again by its width. When you open up the paper, there should be four sections. In the middle of the page, where the sections intersect, students write the word. Starting clockwise, in the first section, students find a definition of the word. The second section includes a sentence they create with the word. The third section is an opportunity to write a synonym or antonym. For words that might not have a clear synonym or antonym, writing a similar word could work ("leg" for "tentacle"). In the last section, students can draw a picture of the word.

It's recommended not to overuse this strategy, so as not to draw students away from the lesson, but it could be useful in order to deeply understand a word.

Have students take notes on other words that cause confusion. Explain that by clicking on the words in red, students can get a quick definition.

# Comprehension support

⮑ *What did we learn in the section called Animals?* (Animals are living things that can move around. All have cells and need to eat food.)

⮑ *Take a look at the section called Food. Did you learn more about your animal or have more wonderings about your animal? Let's add information to the chart.*

⮑ Go through each section, having students collect information or wonderings as they read.

# Collaborative practice ✎

Have students share out the animal they are interested in researching. Consider placing students in small groups based on interest and having the groups work together to research the animal. Have students research their animal—what it eats, how it moves, where it lives, and whether it lays eggs or has live young. Each student can focus on a different part to research. Students can refer to the "What Are Animals?" article as well as their KWL Chart for guidance. Students can also use the resources listed in **Further research** or other library resources. Consider having students share what they've learned with the class.

For further study on the topic, try the activity as a class. Click on the paper and crayon icon in the "What Are Animals?" article, find Activity, and click on Print.

## Differentiation

For **Collaborative practice**, consider having higher-level students compare an animal they researched with another group's animal. They can fill in the Venn Diagram on page 122 with their findings. For students who may require more support, the activity could be adjusted so they are focusing on just one part of the project—such as what the animal eats or how it moves.

## Further research

- PebbleGo includes a variety of articles about animals. Search for Animal Classifications, and click on one of the categories (i.e., About Amphibians, About Birds, etc.) for articles related to that group.

- Amstutz, Lisa, J. *Fish*. My First Animal Kingdom Encyclopedias, North Mankato, Minn.: 2017.

- Amstutz, Lisa, J. *Mammals*. My First Animal Kingdom Encyclopedias, North Mankato, Minn.: 2017.

- Dell, Pamela. *Birds*. My First Animal Kingdom Encyclopedias, North Mankato, Minn.: 2017.

## Standards

**NGSS:**
K-LS1-1, K-ESS3-1, 1-LS1-2

**College and Career Readiness Standards:**
CCSS.ELA-Literacy.CCRA.R.1,
CCSS.ELA-Literacy.CCRA.R.2,
CCSS.ELA-Literacy.CCRA.R.4,
CCSS.ELA-Literacy.CCRA.R.5,
CCSS.ELA-Literacy.CCRA.R.7,
CCSS.ELA-Literacy.CCRA.W.7,
CCSS.ELA-Literacy.CCRA.L.4,
CCSS.ELA-Literacy.CCRA.L.5,
CCSS.ELA-Literacy.CCRA.L.6

**AASL Standards Framework for Learners:**
I.A.1, I.A.2, I.D.1, I.D.2, III.A.1,
III.A.2, III.D.1, V.C.1, VI.A.1

## Materials

- "Group Behavior" PebbleGo article
- Main Idea and Details Sheet, p. 121

# Why do animals behave the way they do?

## Introduce the topic

Start this lesson by playing the two videos located in the PebbleGo article "Group Behavior." The videos can be found in the Media toolbar. Ask students what they notice about the fish and the ants and how these two animals might be similar.

*I heard some of you say the fish were swimming in a group and the ants were also in a group. What did you notice about how the fish were swimming? (Students may say the fish swam in one direction and then they changed direction.) Fish travel in a school, or a group, so they stay safe. Why do you think working in a group is helpful? (Acknowledge and accept student responses.)*

*Animals live in groups in order to survive. They might hunt together, move the things they need from one home to another together, or travel together. We are going to learn more about animal behavior, or the way they act, by reading the PebbleGo article "Group Behavior." As we read, we are going to fill in a Main Idea and Details Sheet. A main idea is the big idea from a text. The details help support the main idea. In the biggest box at the top, we are going to write Animals Survive. In the three boxes after the main idea, we are going to add details from the text to support the main idea. After we read today, we are going to use a chart like this one to select one animal and do more research on its behavior, or why it acts the way it does.*

Depending on the level of support needed, have students read or listen to the article, or read the article to students. The instruction that follows will help to support comprehension of the content as well as connect students to the science topic.

## Vocabulary support

Be on the lookout for vocabulary words that students do not know. Encourage students to share these words with the class. This article includes many names for groups of animals. It may be helpful to create a list of animals and their group name on the board.

*As I was reading this article, I noticed a pattern in it. The article included examples of animals and then it included their group name. Sometimes the article gives the context clue, "groups called [group name]," and sometimes it does not. Let's review some of the sections in the article and write on a list the name of the animal and its group name.* (Write student responses on the board. They'll likely point out the following animals and group names: elephants-herds, wolves-packs, fish-schools, and insects-colonies.) *Sometimes looking for patterns in texts can help us figure out unknown words.*

Have students take notes on other words that cause confusion. Explain that by clicking on the words in red, students can get a quick definition.

## Comprehension support

⇨ *Why do elephants live in herds?* (so elephant mothers can protect their young) *Let's add "Living in groups helps elephants protect their young" as a detail to Animals Survive.*

⇨ *Let's look at the section called Getting Food. How does a pack help a wolf survive? Let's add this detail to our chart.* (By working together, the pack can catch a big animal. Animals get more food this way.)

⇨ Have students collect details about animal survival as they read each section of the article.

## Collaborative practice ✎

Place students in one of four groups, and assign one type of animal behavior to each group: communication, hibernation, migration, or nocturnal animals. Students read the PebbleGo article on that subject in order to share out animal behavior with the group. (Articles can be found by searching for Animal Communication, Hibernation, Migration, and Nocturnal Animals.) Consider providing students with a fresh copy of the chart to fill in new details. Students can add the name of the article to the top box and fill in details about it. Have students refer to the "Group Behavior" Main Idea and Details Sheet for guidance.

For further study on the topic, try the activity as a class. Click on the paper and crayon icon in the "Group Behavior" article, find Activity, and click on Print.

### Differentiation

For **Collaborative practice**, consider placing students in mixed-ability groups and by student interest of the behavior. So that each student is responsible for one part of the research, assign roles. For example, one student could take notes. Student pairs could look for information, and a third student can create a picture of the animal.

### Further research

- PebbleGo "Animal Communication"
- PebbleGo "Hibernation"
- PebbleGo "Migration"
- PebbleGo "Nocturnal Animals"
- Amstutz, Lisa, J. *Fish.* My First Animal Kingdom Encyclopedias, North Mankato, Minn.: 2017.
- Amstutz, Lisa, J. *Mammals.* My First Animal Kingdom Encyclopedias, North Mankato, Minn.: 2017.
- Dunne, Abbie. *Animal Group Behavior.* Life Science. North Mankato, Minn.: Capstone Press, 2017.

## Standards

**NGSS:**
K-LS1-1, K-ESS3-1, 1-LS1-2

**College and Career Readiness Standards:**
CCSS.ELA-Literacy.CCRA.R.1,
CCSS.ELA-Literacy.CCRA.R.2,
CCSS.ELA-Literacy.CCRA.R.4,
CCSS.ELA-Literacy.CCRA.R.7,
CCSS.ELA-Literacy.CCRA.L.4,
CCSS.ELA-Literacy.CCRA.L.5,
CCSS.ELA-Literacy.CCRA.L.6

**AASL Standards Framework for Learners:**
I.A.1, I.A.2, I.D.1, I.D.2, III.A.1, III.A.2, III.D.1, V.C.1, VI.A.1

## Materials

- "About Amphibians" PebbleGo article
- Venn Diagram, p. 122

## Introduce the topic

*Think about some groups that you know about. Our classroom is a group. A youth baseball league is a group. What are some other groups you can think of?* (Acknowledge and accept student responses.) *People, animals, or things are put in a group if they have some things in common. Let's think about our classroom. What makes it a group?* (Acknowledge and accept student responses. Students may say that all children in the class are the same age and from the same area.)

*I heard some of you say that all the students in the class are the same age. Animals are put into groups too. They are classified into groups. To classify means to put into a group and often by similar features. There are different classifications, or groups, of animals: amphibians, birds, fish, mammals, reptiles, and invertebrates. We are going to learn more about one classification of animals today by reading the PebbleGo article "About Amphibians." We are also going to create a Venn diagram about amphibians. Then we will complete the Venn diagram in groups by researching another kind of animal. We'll use the Venn diagram to compare and contrast amphibians to another animal classification. Let's start by labeling the first circle Amphibians and the place where the two circles meet as Both. We'll fill in the second circle with the animal classification we research.*

Depending on the level of support needed, have students read or listen to the article, or read the article to students. The instruction that follows will help to support comprehension of the content as well as connect students to the science topic.

# Vocabulary support

Be on the lookout for vocabulary words that students do not know. Sometimes students will need to sound out a word in order to be able to recognize it.

*When I first came across this word* (point to "mucus" in the Skin section), *I had a hard time reading it. I decided to sound out the word to better understand it. At first, I sounded out the word letter by letter: /m/ /u/ /k/ /u/ /s/. That didn't sound quite right, so I looked for where I could break the word by syllable. I noticed there is an open syllable, so the vowel is long: /mū/. The next syllable is a closed syllable, so the vowel is short: /kus/. Now I can say the word, and I know this word! The word is "mucus." Sometimes sounding out the word can help me recognize it.*

Have students take notes on other words that cause confusion. Explain that by clicking on the words in red, students can get a quick definition.

# Comprehension support

↪ *What did we learn about amphibians in the section called Many Kinds? Can we add this information to our Venn diagram?* (Kinds: salamanders, toads, caecilians)

↪ *In the Habitat section, we learned where amphibians live. What can we add to our diagram about where they live? Is there other information we can add to our diagram?* (Live: on land and in water; cold-blooded)

↪ Have students collect details about amphibians to add to their diagram.

# Collaborative practice ✎

Place students in one of five groups, and assign one animal classification to each group: birds, fish, invertebrates, mammals, and reptiles. Have them write the animal classification as the title of the second circle on the diagram. Students read the PebbleGo article on that topic and fill in the second circle on the Venn diagram with information about it. (Search About Birds, About Fish, About Invertebrates, About Mammals, and About Reptiles.) If the animal classification shares traits with amphibians, instruct students to cross out or erase the information under amphibians and write it in the place where the two circles meet. (Both)

## Differentiation

For **Collaborative practice**, consider having higher-level students draw a third circle on their page and research a new animal. For students requiring additional help, provide them with a KWL Chart (p. 116). Have students fill in what they know and want to know about the animal classification. Then they can fill in what they learned with new information. Students might find it helpful to transfer this information to the Venn diagram.

## Further research

- PebbleGo "About Birds"
- PebbleGo "About Fish"
- PebbleGo "About Invertebrates"
- PebbleGo "About Mammals"
- PebbleGo "About Reptiles"
- Royston, Angela. Animal Classifications Series. Chicago: Heinemann Library, 2015.

**NGSS:**
K-ESS3-1

**College and Career Readiness Standards:**
CCSS.ELA-Literacy.CCRA.R.1,
CCSS.ELA-Literacy.CCRA.R.2,
CCSS.ELA-Literacy.CCRA.R.4,
CCSS.ELA-Literacy.CCRA.L.4,
CCSS.ELA-Literacy.CCRA.L.6

**AASL Standards Framework for Learners:**
I.A.2, I.B.3, I.D.1, I.D.2, I.D.3,
III.A.1, III.A.2, III.D.1, V.C.1,
VI.A.1

**Materials**

- "Painted Lady Butterflies" PebbleGo article
- Making Connections Chart, p. 118
- Students' baby pictures
- Art supplies: construction paper, markers, and crayons

# What is a life cycle?

## Introduce the topic

Invite students to bring in their own baby pictures to class to share. Ask students to notice how much has changed since they were babies.

*Just as we grow up from baby to child to teenager to adult, other living things grow up too. Sometimes an animal just gets bigger. A baby dolphin looks like its parents when it's born. Then it gets bigger. Other times, the animal goes through steps, or stages, to become an adult. Today we are going to learn about the stages painted lady butterflies go through to become adults. Before we begin, let's make connections to the topic. When have you seen a butterfly? What about a caterpillar?* (Acknowledge and accept student responses.)

*As we read the PebbleGo article "Painted Lady Butterflies," we are going to make connections to the text. There are three types of connections. One is a connection we have to ourselves, such as something we may have seen or personally experienced, like seeing a butterfly at the park. Another connection is one we can make to a text we read about the topic. The third connection is a connection to the world. Maybe we watched a TV show about the topic. We'll make connections as we read using a chart.* (Provide a copy of the Making Connections Chart to students, and explain how to use it.) *After we finish reading about butterflies, we'll use our notes to draw a life cycle.*

Depending on the level of support needed, have students read or listen to the article, or read the article to students. The instruction that follows will help to support comprehension of the content as well as connect students to the science topic.

Children often have their own wonderings about life cycles. The **Collaborative practice** could be replaced with research on their own wonderings. Students can also compare and contrast life cycles among living things using the Venn Diagram on page 122.

# Vocabulary support

Be on the lookout for vocabulary words that students do not know. Sometimes there are several unknown words in one paragraph. It may help to try several vocabulary strategies in these situations.

*When I first read the word "metamorphosis" (From Life Cycle), I did not know what it meant. I looked at the sentence for a clue. The sentence says, "Butterflies go through metamorphosis," but I still am unsure what that word means, so I read on. The text says, "Larvae hatch from eggs." I know that larvae are the young of an insect, and they come out of eggs. But I'm still not sure what "metamorphosis" means, and it sounds like it's something butterflies go through. By reading on, I learn that larvae make chrysalises. I am now unsure what the word "chrysalises" means. Sometimes when I read a passage and I'm not sure what a word means, such as metamorphosis, I read on to see if there are clues that provide further meaning. In this case, reading on brought up more unknown words for me. So I decided to click on the word for a definition. By clicking on the word in red, I see a definition that explains the word. It's a series of changes some animals go through as they develop from eggs to adults. This part is about the changes a butterfly goes through to become an adult. By reading on to find clues and using the glossary, I now understand that.*

Have students take notes on other words that cause confusion. Explain that by clicking on the words in red, students can get a quick definition.

# Comprehension support

⟳ *Take a look at the Body section. Are there connections you can make to the information in the text? Add this information to your chart.* (Acknowledge and accept student responses.)

⟳ *What do larvae make when they're ready to grow?* (chrysalises) *Have you ever seen or read about a chrysalis? Include that information in your chart.*

⟳ Have students practice making connections while reading the rest of the article.

# Collaborative practice ✎

Have students work in groups to create a life cycle of a butterfly, using the art supplies. Students can refer to the "Painted Lady Butterflies" article as well as the Making Connections Chart for guidance. Students can also use the resources listed in **Further research** or other library resources. Consider having students share what they've learned with the class.

For further study on the topic, try the activity as a class. Click on the paper and crayon icon in the "Painted Lady Butterflies" article, find Activity, and click on Print.

**Differentiation**

For **Collaborative practice**, consider having students compare and contrast the life stages they go through to a butterfly's life cycle. Using a Venn Diagram (p. 122) would be helpful for this activity. For learners who might require more support, consider showing pictures from the life cycle of a butterfly and going over the stages. You could also show students other kinds of life cycles: plants, frogs, and so on.

**Further research**

- PebbleGo "About Insects"
- PebbleGo "Monarch Butterflies"
- PebbleGo "Frogs"
- Dunn, Mary R. *A Butterfly's Life Cycle.* Explore Life Cycles. North Mankato, Minn.: Capstone Press, 2018.
- Dunn, Mary R. *A Frog's Life Cycle.* Explore Life Cycles. North Mankato, Minn.: Capstone Press, 2018.
- Dunn, Mary R. *A Turtle's Life Cycle.* Explore Life Cycles. North Mankato, Minn.: Capstone Press, 2018.

## Standards

**NGSS:**
K-ESS2-2

**College and Career Readiness Standards:**
CCSS.ELA-Literacy.CCRA.R.1,
CCSS.ELA-Literacy.CCRA.R.2,
CCSS.ELA-Literacy.CCRA.R.4,
CCSS.ELA-Literacy.CCRA.R.5,
CCSS.ELA-Literacy.CCRA.W.7,
CCSS.ELA-Literacy.CCRA.L.4,
CCSS.ELA-Literacy.CCRA.L.6

**AASL Standards Framework for Learners:**
I.A.2, I.B.3, I.D.1, I.D.2, I.D.3,
III.A.1, III.A.2, III.D.1, V.C.1,
V.C.III, VI.A.1

## Materials

- "What Are Germs?" PebbleGo article
- Cause and Effect Chain, p. 123
- Poster board

## Introduce the topic

*What does it feel like to have a cold or the flu?* (Acknowledge and accept student responses.) *Did you know germs cause these illnesses? How do we get a cold or flu?* (Acknowledge and accept student responses.)

*I heard some of you say that germs make people sick, and we catch them from each other. Not all germs are harmful, however. Today we are going to be reading about germs, including the two main types of germs.*

*As we read the PebbleGo article "What Are Germs?," we are going to use a Cause and Effect Chain to take notes. A cause makes something happen. For example, I kicked a ball. My kick is the cause. The ball rolling down the street is the effect. Let's practice giving some causes and effects. What is the effect of being tired?* (sleeping) *What is the cause of a snow day?* (a blizzard or snowy weather)

*After we read, we are going to use our Cause and Effect Chains to come up with a poster for the classroom. The poster will help explain what germs are and give tips for being in a germ-free classroom.*

Depending on the level of support needed, have students read or listen to the article, or read the article to students. The instruction that follows will help to support comprehension of the content as well as connect students to the science topic.

# Vocabulary support

Be on the lookout for vocabulary words that students do not know. Encourage students to share these words with the class. Students can use strategies, such as using picture support, in order to understand the word's meaning.

*I noticed some of you were not sure what the word "microscope" means (From What Are Germs?). Let's take a closer look at the sentence it is in to see if there is a clue, or hint, to its meaning. The sentence says, "They can be seen under a microscope." I now understand a microscope is something you can use to see things, but I'm not exactly sure what it means. I could look at the picture to help me understand. The picture shows a tool that must be a microscope with an image of germs next to it. When I click on the word, I see that it means "an instrument with powerful lenses to magnify very small things," and the picture does show a tool. Looking at the picture and reading its definition helped me figure out the meaning of an unknown word.*

Have students take notes on other words that cause confusion. Explain that by clicking on the words in red, students can get a quick definition.

# Comprehension support

⇨ *What did you learn in the Types of Germs section?* (Bacteria and viruses are two types of germs that can live anywhere. Viruses cause colds.) *What can we add to our Cause and Effect Chain?* (Cause: catching a virus, Effect: common cold or other disease)

⇨ *How do germs spread?* (From person to person) *Where did you find this information?* (How Germs Work). *What can we add to our Cause and Effect Chain?* (Cause: sick person touching the door handle, Effect: next person who touches the handle gets germs; Cause: person touches nose or mouth after touching door handle; Effect: person gets sick)

⇨ Have students find causes and effects as they read the rest of the article.

# Collaborative practice ✐

Have students work in groups to create a poster for the classroom. The poster should include information about what germs are and tips for keeping a germ-free space. Students can refer to the "What Are Germs?" article as well as the Cause and Effect Chain for guidance. Students can also use the resources listed in **Further research** or other library resources. Consider having students share what they've learned with the class.

For further study on the topic, try the activity as a class. Click on the paper and crayon icon in the "What Are Germs?" article, find Activity, and click on Print. Note that the activity is similar to the **Collaborative practice**, but it focuses on the home.

## Differentiation

For **Collaborative practice**, consider having higher-level students think about good germs and how those are used in our world. For learners who might require more support, it may be helpful to break down the assignment by talking about one particular area of the classroom, and what can be done to keep germs at bay.

## Further research

- PebbleGo "Bacteria"
- PebbleGo "Viruses"
- Rustad, Martha E. H. *I Keep Clean*. Healthy Me. North Mankato, Minn.: Capstone Press, 2017.

# Social Studies Lessons

## Standards

**College and Career Readiness Standards:**
CCSS.ELA-Literacy.CCRA.R.1,
CCSS.ELA-Literacy.CCRA.R.2,
CCSS.ELA-Literacy.CCRA.R.4,
CCSS.ELA-Literacy.CCRA.L.4,
CCSS.ELA-Literacy.CCRA.L.6

**AASL Standards Framework for Learners:**
I.A.1, I.A.2, I.B.3, I.D.1, I.D.2,
I.D.3, III.A.1, III.A.2, III.D.1,
V.C.1, VI.A.1

## Materials

- "In My Neighborhood" PebbleGo article
- Question Words Chart, p. 119
- Art supplies: construction paper, markers, and crayons

# What can I find in my neighborhood?

## Introduce the topic

*Think about where you live. The people who live near you are called neighbors. The place where you and your neighbors live is called a neighborhood. It is often filled with the things you need, like a grocery store or a school. In partners, think about your neighborhood. Share with each other the people who live in your neighborhood and the kinds of things that can be found there.* (Walk around as students are talking to hear their discussions. The following could be adjusted based on what you had heard from your students.)

*I heard some of you talk about some of the people in your neighborhood. Others mentioned your family could walk to the library; it's that close. Someone even mentioned a garden that is nearby that provides the neighbors with some fresh vegetables. Today, we are going to learn more about what is in a neighborhood. We are going to read the PebbleGo article "In My Neighborhood." To begin, let's fill in a Question Words Chart. We will use this chart to write down our questions before, during, and after we read the PebbleGo article "In My Neighborhood." Taking notes is a helpful way to keep track of what we learn. We'll also be using our notes when we work in teams to draw our neighborhoods.* (As needed, go over the question words listed on the worksheet.)

*What are some things that should be in a neighborhood? Who works in our neighborhood? What kinds of jobs do they have? Let's write our questions on the chart and then fill in the chart with our answers.* (Model writing down your questions for students in the appropriate spaces.) *What are some other questions we have about what's in a neighborhood that we might find the answers to in the article?* (Acknowledge student responses, filling in the correct part of the chart.)

Depending on the level of support needed, have students read or listen to the article, or read the article to students. The instruction that follows will help to support comprehension of the content as well as connect students to the social studies topic.

# Vocabulary support

Be on the lookout for vocabulary words that students do not know. Encourage students to share these words with the class. Students can use strategies, such as using context clues, in order to understand the word's meaning.

*Some of you had asked what the word "rural" means. Let's take a closer look at the sentence it is in to see if there is a clue, or hint, to its meaning. The sentence says, "But neighborhoods in rural areas are spread out." (From Other Neighborhoods) Are there some clues that will help us figure out the meaning of the word "rural"? The author is telling us rural areas are spread out. I'm still not sure what the meaning is, so I am going to reread this section. In the sentence before this one, the author says big cities are crowded. I think a rural place must be opposite from a city because rural areas are spread out. I'm going to click on the word because the red font tells me the word is linked to a glossary definition. By seeing the definition, I learn that a place is rural if it is "away from cities and towns." Using context clues, or hints around the word, and the glossary helped me figure out the meaning of the word "rural."*

Have students take notes on other words that cause confusion. Explain that by clicking on the words in red, students can get a quick definition.

# Comprehension support

⇨ *What did you learn in the section called My Neighborhood?* (Neighborhoods have places that meet needs. Neighborhoods also have friends.)

⇨ *What kinds of stores can be found in a neighborhood?* (bakery, café, grocery store) *Do you have any new questions after reading Stores in My Neighborhood that you could add to the Question Words Chart?* (Acknowledge and accept student responses.)

⇨ Work through the rest of the tabs. Encourage students to ask questions as they read and to fill in their charts with the questions and answers.

# Collaborative practice ✏

Have students work in partners to create a drawing of their community. It can be a map or a simple drawing, depending on skill level. Students should first talk about their neighborhoods and all of the things that can be found there. Encourage students to list these places. Then have students pick one part of one neighborhood to draw. The pair then shares their drawing, explaining what can be found in the neighborhood. Students can use the activity in the Print toolbar and the Question Words Chart to prepare for the **Collaborative practice**. Click on the paper and crayon icon in the "In My Neighborhood" article, find Share what you know, and click on Print. Students can also use the resources listed in **Further research** during their discussions.

## Differentiation

For **Collaborative practice**, encourage higher-level students to draw a map showing both students' neighborhoods. For learners who might require more support, it might be helpful to have pictures available from different neighborhoods. Learners could select the pictures of things that are available in their communities. For English language learners, consider adding sticky notes to label the pictures.

## Further research

- PebbleGo "In My Home"
- PebbleGo "In My State"
- PebbleGo "In My Town"
- Cane, Ella. *Neighborhoods in My World*. My World. North Mankato, Minn.: 2014.

## Standards

**College and Career Readiness Standards:**
CCSS.ELA-Literacy.CCRA.R.1,
CCSS.ELA-Literacy.CCRA.R.2,
CCSS.ELA-Literacy.CCRA.R.4,
CCSS.ELA-Literacy.CCRA.L.4,
CCSS.ELA-Literacy.CCRA.L.6

**AASL Standards Framework for Learners:**
I.A.2, I.D.1, I.D.2, I.D.3, III.A.1,
III.A.2, III.D.1, V.C.1, VI.A.1

## Materials

- "Games and Fun Then and Now" PebbleGo article

- Timeline, p. 124

# How are the past and present alike? How are they different?

## Introduce the topic

*What are some games that you like to play?* (Encourage students to share out their responses.)

*I heard some of you say that you like to play board games. Others mentioned video games. Do you think your parents played these games when they were young?* (Allow time for students to respond.) *Today we are going to learn more about games throughout time.*

*We are going to read the PebbleGo article "Games and Fun Then and Now." As we read, we are going to fill in a timeline. A timeline is a line that shows events in history by date. The earliest events are placed on the left-hand side of the timeline, and events that happened later are shown to the right. We will use a timeline to take notes as we read the PebbleGo article. Taking notes is a helpful way to keep track of what we learn. We'll use our notes later to come up with interview questions for a parent or caregiver about the games and toys they played with.*

*Take a look at the timeline. In the first box at the top of the line, write Early America.* (Model how to do this for students.) *In the box below that, write 1900s. In the next box on top, write 1950s. In the second box on the bottom of the line, write Today. As we read the article, let's fill in the appropriate box with our findings.*

Depending on the level of support needed, have students read or listen to the article, or read the article to students. The instruction that follows will help to support comprehension of the content as well as connect students to the social studies topic.

# Vocabulary support

Be on the lookout for vocabulary words that students do not know. This article includes a lot of games that might be new to students. Students can use strategies, such as using reference materials, in order to understand the word's meaning. Many of the games listed are in red, so students can find a definition by clicking on the word.

*Some of you had asked what the game "hoop and arrow" means. (From Games on the Frontier) Sometimes a text might not have a clue to its meaning and we have to do further research to find the meaning of that word. In this case, the word is in red, so we can click on it for a definition. By clicking on the word, I learn it's a game American Indians played. They threw an arrow inside a small hoop. By clicking on the word, I learned more about its meaning. What kinds of resources can we use to find out the meanings of unknown words?* (Accept and acknowledge students' responses. They may say a dictionary, an encyclopedia, or a thesaurus.)

Have students take notes on other words that cause confusion. Explain that by clicking on the words in red, students can get a quick definition.

# Comprehension support

⇨ *What kinds of games did children play during colonial America? What kinds of toys did they play with? What about while on the frontier? Let's add these notes to the box that says Early America.* (Colonial America: rolled hoops, spun tops, tag, hopscotch, nine pins, dolls, lacrosse; frontier: I Spy, Fox and Geese, rag dolls, wooden toys, hoop and arrow)

⇨ *When was the teddy bear made?* (during the early 1900s) *Are there games or toys we can add to the timeline for the 1900s?* (stickball, tag, hide and seek, checkers, chess, marbles, crayons, teddy bears)

⇨ Work through the rest of the tabs. Encourage students to ask questions about what they read and to fill in their timelines.

# Collaborative practice ✐

This will be a two-day activity. Encourage students to take their timelines home and talk to a parent or caregiver about the games and toys listed, asking if they played any of the games or with any of the toys. Have students circle the game or toy and write down the year that their parents or caregivers were young and played with it. The next day, encourage groups of students to compare their findings and to share out. Have students talk about which games or toys are the same from history and which are different.

## Differentiation

Encourage student groups to practice with timelines with another article, such as those listed in **Further research**. Encourage all students to note similarities and differences among the dates listed in the timeline. For learners who might require more support, it may be helpful to have pictures available to show how one item has changed through time and to have the child focus on one item. (For example, for "Communication Then and Now," you could provide pictures of how the phone has changed over time.)

## Further research

- PebbleGo "Clothing Then and Now"
- PebbleGo "Communication Then and Now"
- PebbleGo "Farming Then and Now"
- PebbleGo "Homes Then and Now"
- PebbleGo "School Then and Now"
- PebbleGo "Transportation Then and Now"

There is a toolbar of related resources that can be printed (Print toolbar) and another that can be viewed (Media toolbar).

### Print

> Cite icon (pencil and paper): Students may need to reference the article should they be writing a report. They can click on this icon to see the citation as well as highlight it, copy it, and paste it into their report. The citation can also be printed out, placed at learning centers, and used as a reference.

> Article icon (papers): If you'd like to have a printout of the article or the images for center work, click on this icon. Either or both can be printed out.

> Activities icon (crayon and paper): The "Pocahontas" article includes one activity, Share what you know. You can print this out for students to work on. Consider placing it at a center, and encourage students to work collaboratively on the activity.

### Media

> Video icon (TV): Before or after reading the article, encourage students to watch the video for more information about Pocahontas.

> Timeline icon (purple arrow): The timeline shows the major events of the life of Pocahontas, captured in a timeline format. Review how to read a timeline with students by reading the dates and events from left to right. Ask follow-up questions to support comprehension, such as "What happened in 1613?"

# Who was Pocahontas?

Each PebbleGo article has many resources that will help encourage learning about the topic. This lesson explores the resources that appear in the "Pocahontas" article. Encourage students to review these assets in order to answer the question, "Who was Pocahontas?" The format of this lesson may be used to introduce most PebbleGo articles. Some articles may have different asset types.

## Article features

Articles have a number of features that you will want to go over with students.

> Each article provides content by tabs, with each tab on one main idea. With "Pocahontas," there is a tab that introduces the topic and additional tabs on Early Life, Life's Work, Later Years, and Contributions. An activity on exploring main idea and details would be a perfect way to introduce the tabs to students.

> Students can read the article or have it read to them by clicking on the speaker icon.

> Academic terms are highlighted in red. By clicking on the word and the speaker icon, students can read and hear a glossary definition of the word.

> Each tab includes a picture that supports the text.

> The Related Articles for "Pocahontas" are about other influential American Indians during early America.

**College and Career Readiness Standards:**
CCSS.ELA-Literacy.CCRA.R.7,
CCSS.ELA-Literacy.CCRA.R.9

**AASL Standards Framework for Learners:**
I.A.2, I.D.3, VI.A.1

• "Pocahontas" PebbleGo article

# What does the nation celebrate?

## Introduce the topic

Begin the lesson by playing the video located in the Media toolbar.

*During Independence Day, many people like to watch fireworks. What are some other things people like to do during Independence Day?* (Acknowledge and accept student responses.)

*I heard some of you mention picnics and parades are other ways to celebrate. In this lesson, we are going to learn more about Independence Day. Then we will take what we learn to write why the nation celebrates Independence Day. To begin, let's fill in a KWL chart. We will use the KWL Chart to take notes before, during, and after we read the PebbleGo article. Taking notes is a helpful way to keep track of what we know and learn. We can use our notes later when we write about Independence Day.*

*What do we already know about Independence Day? Let's write what we know in the first column.* (Model for students, such as going to parades. Then take some time to write student responses in the first column.) *What do we want to know about Independence Day? Let's write what we want to know in the second column.* (Model for students by writing the question: Why is Independence Day important? Then take some time to write student responses in the second column.)

*Today we are going to read the PebbleGo article "Independence Day." As we read, let's fill in the final column with what we learned.*

Depending on the level of support needed, have students read or listen to the article, or read the article to students. The instruction that follows will help to support comprehension of the content as well as connect students to the social studies topic.

**College and Career Readiness Standards:**
CCSS.ELA-Literacy.CCRA.R.1,
CCSS.ELA-Literacy.CCRA.R.2,
CCSS.ELA-Literacy.CCRA.R.4,
CCSS.ELA-Literacy.CCRA.W.7,
CCSS.ELA-Literacy.CCRA.L.4,
CCSS.ELA-Literacy.CCRA.L.6

**AASL Standards Framework for Learners:**
I.A.2, I.B.3, I.D.1, I.D.2, III.A.1, III.A.2, III.D.1, VI.A.1

**Materials**
- "Independence Day" PebbleGo article
- KWL Chart, p. 116

## Differentiation

For **Collaborative practice**, encourage higher-level students to talk about why the colonists were brave. They could make connections to something else they read on the topic or to something they heard or saw in their world. For learners who might require more support, it might be helpful to discuss the academic vocabulary in the article: "colonists," "declared," "independence," "taxes," and "free." Encourage students to use some of the vocabulary in their writing.

## Further research

- PebbleGo "Declaration of Independence"
- Clay, Kathryn. *The Declaration of Independence.* Introducing Primary Sources. North Mankato, Minn.: Capstone Press, 2018.

# Vocabulary support

Be on the lookout for vocabulary words that students do not know. Sometimes students will need to use multiple strategies in order to understand the word.

*When I first came across this word* (point to "declared" in the What Is It? section), *I had a hard time reading it. At first, I sounded out the word: /d/ /ē/ /kl/ /air/ /d/. Now I can say the word, but I'm still not sure what it means! By clicking on the word, I learn "declare" is "to make known openly or officially." Why might "declared" be a better word choice than "wanted"?* (Acknowledge and accept student responses. They may say that when they declare something, they let everyone know. When they want something, not everyone knows.)

Have students take notes on other words that cause confusion. Explain that by clicking on the words in red, students can get a quick definition.

# Comprehension support

↪ *What did we learn about Independence Day from What Is It? Let's add this information to our chart.* (In 1776, American colonists declared independence from Great Britain.)

↪ *Why did the colonists want to be free?* (The king of England was taxing the colonists.) *What part did we read this in?* (The Story of Independence Day) *Is there anything we can add to our charts?* (Acknowledge and accept student responses.)

↪ Work through the rest of the tabs. Encourage students to add information they learned to their charts.

# Collaborative practice ✎

Have students work in partners to write about why the nation celebrates Independence Day. Students should refer to the article and their KWL Charts for support. They can also use the activity listed in the Print toolbar to take notes. Click on the paper and crayon icon in the "Independence Day" article, find Share what you know, and click on Print. Provide students with additional resources, such as those listed in **Further research**.

# What is a common tradition?

Each PebbleGo article has many resources that will help encourage learning about the topic. This lesson explores the resources that appear in the "Birthdays around the World" article. Encourage students to review these assets in order to answer the question, "What is a common tradition?" The format of this lesson may be used to introduce most PebbleGo articles. Some articles may have different asset types.

## Article features

Articles have a number of features that you will want to go over with students.

➪ Each article provides content by tabs, with each tab on one main idea. With "Birthdays around the World," there are tabs on Birthday Customs, Birthday Food, Birthday Fun, Birthday Presents, and Birthday Luck. An activity on exploring main idea and details would be a perfect way to introduce the tabs to students.

➪ Students can read the article or have it read to them by clicking on the speaker icon.

➪ Academic terms are highlighted in red. By clicking on the word and the speaker icon, students can read as well as hear a glossary definition of the word.

➪ Each tab includes a picture that supports the text.

➪ The related articles for "Birthdays around the World" include "In My Country" and "Games and Fun Then and Now."

## Standards

**College and Career Readiness Standards:** CCSS.ELA-Literacy.CCRA.R.7, CCSS.ELA-Literacy.CCRA.R.9

**AASL Standards Framework for Learners:** I.A.2, I.D.3, VI.A.1

## Materials

• "Birthdays around the World" PebbleGo article

## Toolbars

There is a toolbar of related resources that can be printed (Print toolbar) and another that can be viewed (Media toolbar).

**Print**

❯ Cite icon (pencil and paper): Students may need to reference the article should they be writing a report. They can click on this icon to see the citation as well as highlight it, copy it, and paste it into their report. The citation can also be printed out, placed at learning centers, and used as a reference.

❯ Article icon (papers): If you'd like to have a printout of the article or the images for center work, click on this icon. Either or both can be printed out.

❯ Activities icon (crayon and paper): The "Birthdays around the World" article includes one activity, Share what you know. You can print this out for students to work on. Consider placing it at a center, and encourage students to work collaboratively on the activity.

**Media**

❯ Video icon (TV): Before or after reading the article, encourage students to watch the video for more information about birthdays.

All of the assets included for this article can be used to help students compare and contrast common traditions.

## Standards

**College and Career Readiness Standards:**
CCSS.ELA-Literacy.CCRA.R.1,
CCSS.ELA-Literacy.CCRA.R.2,
CCSS.ELA-Literacy.CCRA.R.4,
CCSS.ELA-Literacy.CCRA.W.7,
CCSS.ELA-Literacy.CCRA.L.4,
CCSS.ELA-Literacy.CCRA.L.6

**AASL Standards Framework for Learners:**
I.A.2, I.D.1, I.D.2, III.A.1, III.A.2, III.D.1, VI.A.1

## Materials

- "Games around the World" PebbleGo article
- T-Chart, p. 117

# What is culture?

## Introduce the topic

*Have you ever gone to a restaurant with food that you never had before? What kind of food did you have?* (Acknowledge and accept student responses.)

*I heard some of you mention some foods from other countries. Each country has a rich culture. Culture is a people's way of life. It includes things like art, customs, and traditions. What are some customs and traditions that we have?* (Acknowledge and accept student responses.)

*I heard some of you talk about some of the holidays we celebrate. Others talked about some of the food we make. Culture includes things like food, clothing, holidays, games, language, and so much more. In this lesson, we are going to learn more about culture by reading about games played around the world. Then we are going to select one place, research it, and write about the culture of the people from that place. We will use a T-Chart to take notes before and after we read the PebbleGo article. Taking notes is a helpful way to keep track of what we know and learn. We can use our notes later when we write about one culture.*

*Let's title the first column Place, and we'll title the second column Examples of Culture. Today we are going to read the PebbleGo article "Games around the World." As we read, let's fill in the T-Chart with our findings.*

Depending on the level of support needed, have students read or listen to the article, or read the article to students. The instruction that follows will help to support comprehension of the content as well as connect students to the social studies topic.

# Vocabulary support

Be on the lookout for vocabulary words that students do not know. Encourage students to share these words with the class. The following is a model on using multiple strategies.

*As I was reading, I wasn't sure what "worldwide" meant. (From Playing Games) Let's take a closer look at the sentence it is in to see if there is a clue, or hint, to its meaning. The sentence says, "Others are popular worldwide." I'm not sure what the meaning of the word is from this sentence, so I reread the sentence before it. This sentence says, "Some games are popular in just one place." The phrase, "one place," gives me a clue. It tells me that the game is popular in just one place, but then the next sentence draws this idea out. Other games are popular elsewhere—worldwide. By looking at "worldwide," I notice it is one word that is made up of two smaller words: "world" and "wide." I know both of these words, so "worldwide" must mean around the world. By using context clues and by studying and breaking apart the word, I was able to understand its meaning.*

Have students take notes on other words that cause confusion. Explain that by clicking on the words in red, students can get a quick definition.

# Comprehension support

↪ *What did we learn about board games? Can we add this information to our charts?* (South Korea: Yut; Kenya and Russia: Chess)

↪ *Where are sports popular?* (Almost everywhere) *Did anything surprise you about this section?* (Acknowledge and accept student responses.)

↪ Work through the rest of the tabs. Encourage students to add information they learned to their T-Charts. *Are games an important part of a people's culture? Explain why or why not.* (Acknowledge and accept student responses. If they are unsure, explain that games are a part of their life.)

↪ *Are any of the games mentioned in the article also played here? Which ones do you play?* (Acknowledge and accept student responses.)

# Collaborative practice 🖉

Have students work in partners to research the culture in a place and find three examples of it in use. Students should refer to the article and their T-Charts for support. Provide students with additional resources, such as those listed in **Further research**. Have students write a paragraph about their findings and share out with the group.

## Differentiation

For **Collaborative practice**, encourage students to work in mixed-ability groups and to share what they learned from their research. For learners who might require more support, it may be helpful to compare, by way of pictures, examples of culture in another place with those here.

## Further research

- PebbleGo "Afghanistan"
- PebbleGo "India"
- PebbleGo "Mexico"
- Clapper, Nikki Bruno. *Let's Look at Cuba.* Let's Look at Countries. North Mankato, Minn.: Capstone Press, 2018.
- Clapper, Nikki Bruno. *Let's Look at Greece.* Let's Look at Countries. North Mankato, Minn.: Capstone Press, 2018.

# Who helped shape the United States?

## Introduce the topic

*Who are some leaders that you know about? Are there any leaders in our school?* (Acknowledge and accept student responses.) *I heard some of you say that the president of the United States is a leader as is the principal.*

*What do leaders do?* (Acknowledge and accept student responses.) *Leaders help lead a group of people. They help make rules and laws that will protect people and keep them safe. They also help shape the community. That can mean making the community a better place to be. Our principal helps shape our school community by encouraging school spirit. Think about a leader from the past or present that you know about. How did that person help shape the community?* (Acknowledge and accept student responses.)

*In this lesson, we are going to learn more about one leader from long ago and how he shaped the United States of America. We will use a Three Column Chart to take notes as we read the PebbleGo article. Taking notes is a helpful way to keep track of what we know and learn. We can use our notes later when we write a letter to a leader who helped shape the United States or our community.*

*Let's title the first column Leader, and we'll title the second column Event in History. Then let's title the last column What the Leader Did. Today we are going to read the PebbleGo article "Abraham Lincoln." As we read, let's fill in the Three Column Chart with our findings.*

Depending on the level of support needed, have students read or listen to the article, or read the article to students. The instruction that follows will help to support comprehension of the content as well as connect students to the social studies topic.

# Vocabulary support

Be on the lookout for vocabulary words that students do not know. Encourage students to share these words with the class. The following is a model on using the glossary to look up unknown words.

*Some of you had asked me what "elected" means. (From Life's Work) Let's take a closer look at the sentence it is in to see if there is a clue, or hint, to its meaning. The sentence says, "In 1846 he was elected to the U.S. Congress." It seems like there's a connection between "elected" and "U.S. Congress." But I'm still not sure what the word means. I can use the glossary to look up the word "elect." I learn it means "to choose someone as a leader by voting." What do you think the word "elected" means in this sentence based on the definition? (Wait for student responses.) That's right, Lincoln was chosen to be part of the U.S. Congress. By looking it up in the glossary, I learned what "elected" means.*

Have students take notes on other words that cause confusion. Explain that by clicking on the words in red, students can get a quick definition.

# Comprehension support

⇨ *What did we learn about Lincoln in the parts called Introduction and Early Life? Was there anything from his early life that helped him become a leader?* (Lincoln was the 16th president. Students may say he had an interest in reading and he helped run a store, which may have helped prepare him to become a leader.)

⇨ *We learn that some important historical events happened during Lincoln's life. What do we learn about these historical events from reading Life's Work and Last Years?* (States fought about slavery and states' rights. Lincoln signed a paper to end slavery. John Wilkes Booth killed Lincoln.) *Let's think about where we can add this information to the Three Column Chart.*

⇨ *How did Lincoln help shape the United States? Let's add this to our chart.* (Lincoln helped end slavery.)

⇨ *What made Lincoln a good leader?* (From Contributions tab; Students may say he helped end slavery and that he kept the United States as one country.)

# Collaborative practice ✎

Explain to students that they are going to write a letter to a leader, from the past or present, thanking him or her for his or her work. Students can choose to write to Abraham Lincoln, or they can research another leader or write to a local leader. Have students work in partners on this project. Encourage students to continue to take notes on the Three Column Chart. Provide students with additional resources, such as those listed in **Further research**. Have students share their letters with the group. You may also want to go over the parts of a letter with students.

## Differentiation

For **Collaborative practice**, encourage all students to think about how the leader they chose helped shape the United States or the local community. For learners who might require more support, it may be helpful to discuss the leader and how his or her contributions helped the nation and/or community. Encourage group discussion about the leader, and provide the opportunity and time for students to share their thoughts and build off of one another.

## Further research

- See the PebbleGo articles for Presidents and First Ladies
- See the PebbleGo articles for Civil Rights Leaders
- See the PebbleGo articles for Biographies
- Schuck, Donald L., and Bruce Bednarchuk. America's Leaders Series. North Mankato, Minn.: Cantata Learning, 2015.

# Why is government important?

## Introduce the topic

This lesson is about state elected leaders rather than national leaders so as to connect students to local government. The lesson could be adjusted to focus on national leaders.

*Just like the national government makes decisions for the country, there are people who help make decisions for each state. Today we are going to be learning about one type of state leader—the governor. What kinds of issues happen in our state? Let's make a list.* (Write on the board or chart paper as students call out ideas.)

*I heard some of you say that roads might be a state issue. The other day I was driving on one of the roads and noticed a pothole. That is something the state will need to fix.*

*Local government has a lot of items to oversee—from roads and schools to taxes too. As we read about the job of governor, we are going to fill in a KWL Chart. In the first column, let's fill in what we already know about governors.* (Take notes as students call out answers. They may say that governors are local or help make decisions for the state.) *Let's fill in what we want to know in the second column.* (Help promote discussion by providing one of your wonderings, such as wondering who can be governor.) *As we read, we will fill in the final column with information that we have learned. We will use our chart later on to write a letter to the governor, asking for help on a local project.*

Depending on the level of support needed, have students read or listen to the article, or read the article to students. The instruction that follows will help to support comprehension of the content as well as connect students to the social studies topic.

## Vocabulary support

Be on the lookout for vocabulary words that students do not know. Encourage students to share these words with the class. The following is a model on using context clues to better understand words.

*As I was reading, I came across the word "veto." (From The Governor's Job) I'm not quite sure what it means. Let's take a closer look at the sentence it is in to see if there is a clue, or hint, to its meaning. The sentence says, "They sign bills into laws or veto them." It seems like there's a connection between "they sign bills into laws" and "or veto them." If governors are signing bills into laws, they approve the laws and everyone needs to follow the laws. I think "veto" means the opposite. The word "or" in the sentence is a clue that it means the opposite. If governors veto a bill, that must mean they don't approve the bill and it doesn't become a law. By looking at context clues, I was able to figure out that "veto" means the opposite of signing a bill into law.*

Have students take notes on other words that cause confusion. Explain that by clicking on the words in red, students can get a quick definition.

# Comprehension support

↪ *Governors have a lot of responsibilities! What kinds of responsibilities did we learn about in the section called The Governor's Job?* (Governors are in charge of signing bills into laws, the states' military, sharing ideas on how to spend money, and choosing state leaders.) *Was any of this information new to you? Let's add it to the chart.*

↪ *I learned some important information on who can be governor in the section called Who Can Be Governor?, so I will add it to my chart. Why do you think a governor must live in the state he or she serves?* (An inference will need to be made here. Students may say the governor needs to live in the same state he or she serves in so that he or she understands the local issues.)

↪ *People vote for the governor. What do you think happens if people like their governor?* (People will reelect him or her.)

↪ *Take a look at the section called The Governor's Duties. What kinds of decision does the governor make along with other state lawmakers?* (How to spend money)

↪ *Was there any information that was new to you as you read this article? Add it to your chart.* (Acknowledge and accept student responses.)

# Collaborative practice ✐

As a class, come up with a list of issues or concerns that you would like local government to take action on. This might include fixing some of the roads or building a new park. Discuss what the letter should include, such as what the issue is, evidence that it is an issue, and ideas for the fix. Encourage students to come up with personal stories about the issue or evidence that it is a problem. Then craft the letter together as a class. You may wish to take some time to discuss the elements of a letter. Review the KWL Chart as needed.

## Differentiation

Encourage higher-level students to think about other local offices, such as the mayor or elected representatives. See the resources listed by **Further research** for ideas. Encourage students to fill out another KWL Chart as they read about this elected official. For students who might require support, further break down the **Collaborative practice**. Click on the paper and crayon icon in the "Governor" article, find Share what you know, and click on Print. Then fill out the worksheet as a small group.

## Further research

- PebbleGo "City Council"
- PebbleGo "Mayor"
- Manning, Jack. *The City Mayor*. Our Government. North Mankato, Minn.: Capstone Press, 2015.
- Manning, Jack. *The State Governor*. Our Government. North Mankato, Minn.: Capstone Press, 2015.

**College and Career Readiness Standards:**
CCSS.ELA-Literacy.CCRA.R.1,
CCSS.ELA-Literacy.CCRA.R.2,
CCSS.ELA-Literacy.CCRA.R.4,
CCSS.ELA-Literacy.CCRA.L.4,
CCSS.ELA-Literacy.CCRA.L.6

**AASL Standards Framework for Learners:**
I.A.2, I.B.3, I.D.1, I.D.2, I.D.3, II.C.1, III.A.1, III.A.2, III.D.1, V.C.2, VI.A.1

## Materials

- "Responsibility" PebbleGo article
- Main Idea and Details Sheet, p. 121
- Poster board

# What are our responsibilities?

## Introduce the topic

This lesson is a perfect way to begin the school year, as students discuss responsibilities, which could be a tie-in to class rules.

*Who knows what the word "responsibility" means?* (Allow time for students to respond. Then build on each idea students suggest.) *I heard some of you say that being responsible means keeping a promise. Others mentioned work they are supposed to do at home, like chores. Being responsible means keeping a promise and doing the work you're supposed to do. What are some responsibilities you have at home and in class?* (Consider making a list as students call out their responsibilities.)

*Wow! I am impressed by all of the things for which you are responsible. Today we are going to read the PebbleGo article "Responsibility." As we read, we are going to fill in a Main Idea and Details Sheet. The main idea is Ways We Are Responsible. We are going to learn details that give more information about the main idea. We will add those details to our chart. After we read the article, we'll take what we learn to come up with a Classroom Responsibility Chart.*

Depending on the level of support needed, have students read or listen to the article, or read the article to students. The instruction that follows will help to support comprehension of the content as well as connect students to the social studies topic.

## Vocabulary support

Be on the lookout for vocabulary words that students do not know. Encourage students to share these words with the class. Students can use strategies, such as using context clues, in order to understand the word's meaning.

*As I came across this word* (point to the word "recycle" in the Responsibility Around Town section), *I was not sure what it meant. The sentence says, "Put trash in a garbage can and recycle." Let's take a closer look at the sentence it is in to see if there is a clue, or hint, to its meaning. I think the word "trash" is related to "recycle." Some things get thrown away. But some things are put somewhere else. I notice that we have a bin at home for things that can be reused for other products. I think "recycle" means to make older things into newer things. I can click on the word to get a definition. By using context clues and the glossary, I learned what the word "recycle" means.*

Have students take notes on other words that cause confusion. Explain that by clicking on the words in red, students can get a quick definition.

# Comprehension support

⟳ *What did we learn about responsibility at school? Let's add these details to the first Details box.* (completing work on time, being on time for class, keeping track of school supplies) *Are these responsibilities true for you?* (Acknowledge and accept student responses.)

⟳ *Let's take a closer look at the section called Responsibility at Home. What does it mean to own up to our mistakes?* (Students may say it means taking responsibility for their actions.) *What are some responsibilities at home? Let's add details to our chart. We'll add them to the second Details box.* (doing chores, taking care of a pet, owning mistakes)

⟳ Go through the remaining tabs, adding details to the chart.

⟳ *Why is it important to be responsible?* (So we can be trusted and so we can set a good example for others.) *Where did you read this information?* (Why Responsibility Matters)

# Collaborative practice ✏

Explain to students that they are going to work in a group to think about ways that they can be responsible in the classroom. They will use their Main Idea and Details Sheet, the materials listed in **Further research**, and discussion to come up with ideas. Students then share out their ideas so they can be added to a Classroom Responsibility Chart.

## Differentiation

For **Collaborative practice**, encourage higher-level students to write about how they can be responsible in the community. For learners who might require more support, consider having them circle one of the items on their graphic organizers to flesh out. For example, for keeping track of school supplies, students can identify where the materials should go in the classroom.

## Further research

- PebbleGo "Leadership"
- PebbleGo "Self-Discipline"
- Higgins, Melissa. *I Am Responsible*. I Don't Bully. North Mankato, Minn.: Capstone Press, 2014.
- Higgins, Melissa. *I Am Trustworthy*. I Don't Bully. North Mankato, Minn.: Capstone Press, 2014.

## Standards

**College and Career Readiness Standards:**
CCSS.ELA-Literacy.CCRA.R.1,
CCSS.ELA-Literacy.CCRA.R.2,
CCSS.ELA-Literacy.CCRA.R.4,
CCSS.ELA-Literacy.CCRA.L.4,
CCSS.ELA-Literacy.CCRA.L.6

**AASL Standards Framework for Learners:**
I.A.2, I.B.1, I.D.1, I.D.2, I.D.3,
III.A.1, III.A.2, III.D.1, IV.A.3,
V.C.2, VI.A.1

## Materials

- "Doctors" PebbleGo article
- T-Chart, p. 117

# What jobs are in my community?

## Introduce the topic

There are times when children may have misconceptions about what is fact. The basis for these misconceptions is their own experiences. For example, a child might think that because a parent is a dentist, there is a dentist in every community. This activity is meant to help students rely on a few sources in order to determine what is a fact.

*What does "community" mean?* (Allow time for students to respond.) *I heard some of you say a community is a place where you live. Communities also include neighbors. Sometimes, a community includes different kinds of jobs. Are there stores in your community? What do the stores sell?* (Acknowledge and accept student responses.)

*In addition to stores, sometimes there are people who provide services in a community. Services are work done for another person, like mowing the lawn or cleaning your teeth. Today we are going read about doctors. Doctors provide many types of services. As we read, we are going to fill in a T-Chart. Let's label the first column of the T-Chart with Service, and we'll label the second column of the chart In Our Community. As we read, we're going to write the kind of service that doctors give in the first column. Then we will add an "X" to the second column if the service is in your community. You can talk to each other as well as caregivers about whether these services are in the community. Then we'll come back as a group and talk about what kinds of services are in the community.*

Depending on the level of support needed, have students read or listen to the article, or read the article to students. The instruction that follows will help to support comprehension of the content as well as connect students to the social studies topic.

# Vocabulary support

Be on the lookout for vocabulary words that students do not know. Encourage students to share these words with the class. Students can use strategies, such as using a glossary and dictionary, in order to understand the word's meaning.

*We came across a word that a lot of you asked about. The word is "scrubs," and it was in the section called Clothing. We know that the word has something to do with clothing. Let's take a closer look at the sentence to see if we can figure out the meaning. The sentence says, "Some doctors wear scrubs." After reading this sentence, I understand it's something doctors wear, but I'm still not sure what the word means. Sometimes if we come across an unknown word, it's helpful to seek out another reference, like the glossary. By clicking on the word, I learn a little that scrubs include shirts and pants worn by doctors and nurses. By looking up the word in a dictionary, I learn that scrubs are loose, light-fitting uniforms that doctors wear in hospitals. Looking up the definition of "scrubs" helped me understand the word better.*

Have students take notes on other words that cause confusion. Explain that by clicking on the words in red, students can get a quick definition.

# Comprehension support

⤷ *After reading the section called Doctors, what did we learn about the services they provide? (Doctors help the sick, treat people, prevent people from becoming sick, and give people checkups.) Let's add these services to the T-Chart. Do you know whether these services are provided in your community? If you're not sure, it's OK to add an "X" later, after talking to a parent or caregiver.*

⤷ *We learn that doctors work in hospitals and clinics. Let's add those details to our chart. Let's add an "X" to the chart if there are hospitals and clinics in the community.*

⤷ Go through the remaining tabs, adding details to the chart.

⤷ *There's not just one kind of doctor, but many kinds. Dentists are a kind of doctor. What kinds of doctors and services do you know about? Let's add those to our charts. We'll also add an "X" if the doctor is in the community.*

# Collaborative practice ✏

This **Collaborative practice** could take two days. Explain to students that they are going to work in a group to read about one other kind of job in the community. They will add on to the T-Chart with services the worker provides. Then they will discuss whether that job exists in their community, adding an "X" next to the service if so. They can also bring the chart home to discuss with a parent or caregiver. Provide students with additional resources, such as those listed in **Further research**. Have students share out about whether there are some jobs listed in the article that don't exist in the community and discuss the jobs that do exist in the community.

## Differentiation

For **Collaborative practice**, encourage all students to share what they've learned and whether there is a job they'd like to do someday. For students requiring extra support, it might be helpful to work through the PebbleGo article "In My Neighborhood." Discuss whether the people and places referenced in the article are in their neighborhood.

## Further research

- PebbleGo "Construction Workers"
- PebbleGo "Dentists"
- PebbleGo "Garbage Collectors"
- PebbleGo "Teachers"

## Standards

**College and Career Readiness Standards:**
CCSS.ELA-Literacy.CCRA.R.1,
CCSS.ELA-Literacy.CCRA.R.2,
CCSS.ELA-Literacy.CCRA.R.4,
CCSS.ELA-Literacy.CCRA.L.4,
CCSS.ELA-Literacy.CCRA.L.6

**AASL Standards Framework for Learners:**
I.A.1, I.A.2, I.B.1, I.D.1, I.D.2, I.D.3, II.C.1, III.A.1, III.A.2, III.D.1, VI.A.1

## Materials

- "What Is Money?" PebbleGo article
- Making Connections Chart, p. 118
- Store advertisements (grocery and clothing stores)
- Calculators
- Chart paper

## Introduce the topic

*What kinds of things do we pay for with money?* (Acknowledge and accept student responses.)

*I heard some of you say that we pay for toys and clothes with money. Money is used for all kinds of things—from grocery shopping to paying for a visit to the doctor. What do you think happened before money was around?* (Acknowledge and accept student responses.)

*Did you know that long ago, people used other things like shells, beads, and stones for money? How do you think people used these things?* (Acknowledge and accept student responses.) *That's right, people traded with these things.*

*Today we are going to make connections as we read. Some of the connections we have to a text are things we can connect to another text. Maybe you've already read about the topic of money in another book. A second kind of connection is making a connection to ourselves. Some of the topics we read about we may have seen or experienced. The final connection is to our world. This means we've heard about the topic in our world, such as on TV.*

*Today we are going to read the PebbleGo article "What Is Money?" As we read, let's fill in the Making Connections Chart with connections we can make. Then we are going to use what we learn to do a project on why we need money.*

Depending on the level of support needed, have students read or listen to the article, or read the article to students. The instruction that follows will help to support comprehension of the content as well as connect students to the social studies topic.

# Vocabulary support

Be on the lookout for vocabulary words that students do not know. Encourage students to share these words with the class. Some of the words include a definition within the sentence, which might be a helpful lesson for students.

*As I was reading, I came across a word—"currency." (From Money around the World) I was not sure what the word meant. Let's take a closer look at the sentence it is in to see if there is a clue, or hint, to its meaning. The sentence says, "The money each country uses is called currency." The author is giving us a definition of the word within the sentence. I noticed when I clicked on the word "currency" and saw the definition, it was the same as the sentence. Authors sometimes include the definition of a word in the sentence. Sometimes they do it to help us understand a tricky concept.*

Have students take notes on other words that cause confusion. Explain that by clicking on the words in red, students can get a quick definition.

# Comprehension support

⇨ *What is something you learned as you read the section called Money? Is there a connection you can make to this section? Let's add it to our charts.* (Acknowledge and accept student responses.)

⇨ *When might you have used coins to pay for something? Let's add that information to our charts.*

⇨ *What kind of connection can you make to how bills are made? Why might coins be stamped with designs?* (Students will need to make an inference for the second question. They may say coins are stamped so the different types are clear.) *Why do you think people use coins?* (Students may say to pay for things that cost less than a dollar.)

⇨ Have students make connections to the sections that remain.

# Collaborative practice ✎

With this practice, students will have a better understanding of money. Have students work in groups. Tell them that today they are going to plan a list of items they want to buy with $20. Then they should use the store advertisements to identify the cost of each item. Provide calculators so they can tally up the costs.

This activity could work by providing students with the ads first, and then having students come up with their list. Encourage students to discuss what they will need to cross off the list if they are over $20.

## Differentiation

For **Collaborative practice**, encourage higher-level students to write about their shopping choices and why they made them. For learners who might require more support, consider having a discussion about the different types of money, and what can be bought with each type. It will be helpful to use play money during this conversation. It may be necessary with younger students to complete this activity as a group.

## Further research

- PebbleGo "Earning Money"
- PebbleGo "Needs and Wants"
- Reina, Mary. *Learn About Money.* Money and You. North Mankato, Minn.: Capstone Press, 2015.

## Standards

**College and Career Readiness Standards:**
CCSS.ELA-Literacy.CCRA.R.1,
CCSS.ELA-Literacy.CCRA.R.2,
CCSS.ELA-Literacy.CCRA.R.4,
CCSS.ELA-Literacy.CCRA.L.4,
CCSS.ELA-Literacy.CCRA.L.6

**AASL Standards Framework for Learners:**
I.A.2, I.D.1, I.D.2, I.D.3, II.C.1, III.A.1, III.A.2, III.D.1, VI.A.1

## Materials

- "Needs and Wants" PebbleGo article
- T-Chart, p. 117
- Store advertisements (grocery, clothing, toy, furniture, etc.)
- Chart paper

# What is the difference between a need and a want?

## Introduce the topic

This lesson covers needs and wants. Students may find it tricky to discern a need from a want. Be sure to focus on needs for survival, such as healthful food, shelter, and keeping warm, in order to help differentiate between needs and wants.

*What are some things we need in order to stay alive?* (Acknowledge and accept student responses.)

*That's right! We need food and water to survive. We also need a place to live and to keep warm. Needs are things that help us to survive. Now that we know what needs are, what are wants?* (Acknowledge and accept student responses.)

*I heard some of you say wants are things that are nice to have but we don't need to have. What are some examples?* (Acknowledge and accept student responses. Write them on the board as students share out. Students may mention toys and candy as wants.)

*You came up with lots of wants. Today we are going to learn more about this topic by reading the PebbleGo article "Needs and Wants." As we read, we will fill out a T-Chart. Let's label the first column of the T-Chart Needs and the second column Wants. Then we are going to use what we learn to do a class project on needs and wants.*

Depending on the level of support needed, have students read or listen to the article, or read the article to students. The instruction that follows will help to support comprehension of the content as well as connect students to the social studies topic.

# Vocabulary support

Be on the lookout for vocabulary words that students do not know. Encourage students to share these words with the class. Students may need support decoding some of the words. This lesson provides such support.

*Sometimes we come across words that we're not sure how to read. It helps to sound out the word in these situations. I see a word here that could be difficult to read. (Point to the word "choices" in the Making Choices section.) We've learned some of the sounds for these letters. Let's try putting the sounds together. What sound do the first two letters make? (/ch/) That's right, the /ch/ sound. The next two vowels make one sound. They make the /oy/ sound. Let's say it together: /ch//oy/. The next letter is a soft c. Sometimes the c is hard, like "cat." And sometimes it's soft like "city." Now we can put the letters together: /ch//oy//s/. I also see an -es at the end of the word, so we know the word is plural. Let's say the word together: "choices." What do you think choices are? (Acknowledge and accept student responses.) That's right, choices are what's picked between or among a few things.*

Have students take notes on other words that cause confusion. Explain that by clicking on the words in red, students can get a quick definition.

# Comprehension support

➦ *Where is a place people buy something they need? What about a want?* (Acknowledge and accept student responses. Students will likely say people purchase things they need at grocery stores and things they want at malls.) *In which section did you read this information?* (Spending Money)

➦ *Let's take a look at the sections called What Are Needs? and What Are Wants? What can we add to our T-Chart in the Needs and Wants columns?* (Needs: food, clothing, a place to live; Wants: bicycles, toys, movies)

➦ *Sometimes it can be hard to tell the difference between a need and a want. Did the text talk about this? How might we add this information to our T-Charts?* (Students may say that food is a need, and candy is a food, but there are more healthful food choices. This information appears in Telling Needs and Wants Apart.)

➦ *When is it OK to spend money on a want?* (Students may say that when people have met all of their needs and have some money left over. Allow students to discuss this topic and build on each other's ideas.)

# Collaborative practice ✐

As a class, create a collage of needs and wants. Use chart paper labeled with Needs and Wants. Then encourage students to cut out pictures of products from different kinds of advertisements: clothing, food, toys, and so on. Encourage students to post all pictures they deem as a need or a want. Do not discourage them from posting a picture. After all items are posted, discuss the choices. Ask whether there are items on the chart that are really a want, not a need. Encourage students to voice their arguments for or against a product. The articles and books listed in **Further research** may be of assistance during this project.

## Differentiation

For **Collaborative practice**, encourage higher-level students to write about their argument for why they chose something as a need. For learners who might require more support, consider having them fill out the Share what you know worksheet before finding needs and wants. The activity can be found by clicking on the crayon icon in the Print toolbar. The worksheet will allow students the opportunity to come up with facts about needs and wants.

## Further research

- PebbleGo "Goods and Services"
- PebbleGo "Making Choices"
- Staniford, Linda. Wants versus Needs Series. Chicago: Heinemann Library, 2015.

**Social Studies Lessons:** What is the difference between a need and a want?

83

# What are goods and services?

## Toolbars

There is a toolbar of related resources that can be printed (Print toolbar) and another that can be viewed (Media toolbar).

### Print

> Cite icon (pencil and paper): Students may need to reference the article should they be writing a report. They can click on this icon to see the citation as well as highlight it, copy it, and paste it into their report. The citation can also be printed out, placed at learning centers, and used as a reference.

> Article icon (papers): If you'd like to have a printout of the article or the images for center work, click on this icon. Either or both can be printed out.

> Activities icon (crayon and paper): The "Goods and Services" article includes one activity, Share what you know. You can print this out for students to work on. Consider placing it at a center, and encourage students to work collaboratively on the activity.

### Media

> Video icon (TV): Before or after reading the article, encourage students to watch the video for more information about goods and services.

All of the assets included for this article can be used to help better understand what goods and services are.

Each PebbleGo article has many resources that will help encourage learning about the topic. This lesson explores the resources that appear in the "Goods and Services" article. Encourage students to review these assets in order to answer the question, "What are goods and services?" The format of this lesson may be used to introduce most PebbleGo articles. Some articles may have different asset types.

## Article features

Articles have a number of features that you will want to go over with students.

> Each article provides content by tabs, with each tab on one main idea. With "Goods and Services," there is a tab that introduces the topic called Buying Things and additional tabs on What Are Goods?, What Are Services?, Producers, and Consumers. An activity on exploring main idea and details would be a perfect way to introduce the tabs to students.

> Students can read the article or have it read to them by clicking on the speaker icon.

> Academic terms are highlighted in red. By clicking on the word and the speaker icon, students can read as well as hear a glossary definition of the word.

> Each tab includes a picture that supports the text.

> The related articles for "Goods and Services" include "Needs and Wants" and "Consumers and Producers."

### Standards

**College and Career Readiness Standards:** CCSS.ELA-Literacy.CCRA.R.7, CCSS.ELA-Literacy.CCRA.R.9

**AASL Standards Framework for Learners:** I.A.2, I.D.3, VI.A.1

### Materials

- "Goods and Services" PebbleGo article

# How do I use a map?

## Introduce the topic

*Imagine that you could fly. What kinds of things would you see below you?* (Acknowledge and accept student responses.)

*A map is a type of tool that shows where things are located from up above. There are different kinds of maps to show different things. Some maps show where each country or each state might be. Some maps give lots of information about land features. And some maps just show a neighborhood.*

*A while ago, people used paper maps when they traveled. Now people might use an app on their phones for directions. Why are maps helpful?* (Acknowledge and accept student responses.)

*Someone had mentioned that a map is helpful to get from one place to another. Today we are going to learn more about maps. We are also going to be making inferences as we read. Sometimes a text doesn't provide all the information on a topic. Using information in the text plus what we already know to figure out something is called inferring.*

*Today we are going to read the PebbleGo article "What Is a Map?" We are going to use a Making Inferences Chart to take notes as we read. I will ask you questions as we read. In the first column, you will write clues from the text. In the second column, you will write what you already know about the topic. Then you'll use both of those pieces of information to make an inference. We are going to use this information as we make our own maps.*

Depending on the level of support needed, have students read or listen to the article, or read the article to students. The instruction that follows will help to support comprehension of the content as well as connect students to the social studies topic.

## Vocabulary support

Be on the lookout for vocabulary words that students do not know. Encourage students to share these words with the class. Students may need support reading some of the words. This lesson provides support on using multiple strategies (visualizing and looking up the word in the glossary) in order to better understand an unknown word.

### Standards

**College and Career Readiness Standards:**
CCSS.ELA-Literacy.CCRA.R.1,
CCSS.ELA-Literacy.CCRA.R.2,
CCSS.ELA-Literacy.CCRA.R.4,
CCSS.ELA-Literacy.CCRA.L.4,
CCSS.ELA-Literacy.CCRA.L.6

**AASL Standards Framework for Learners:**
I.A.1, I.A.2, I.B.3, I.D.1, I.D.2, I.D.3, III.A.1, III.A.2, III.D.1, VI.A.1

### Materials

- "What Is a Map?" PebbleGo article
- Making Inferences Chart, p. 120

**Further research**

- PebbleGo "Map Directions"
- PebbleGo "Map Symbols and Keys"
- Brennan, Linda Crotta. *Maps: What You Need to Know.* Fact Files. North Mankato, Minn.: Capstone Press, 2018.

*I often like to visualize what I'm reading so I can better understand the text. Visualizing means I create a picture in my mind of what I am reading. Visualizing the text also helps me understand unknown words. For example, as I was reading, I stopped at the word "carved." (From History) I wasn't entirely sure what that meant. I reread the sentence it was in: "The oldest maps were carved in stone." I am able to make a picture in my mind of people making maps in stone. Stone is a hard material, so "carve" must have something to do with how the maps were made. When I click on the word, I get a definition, and I learn that "carve" is to cut. It would make sense that people made maps by cutting into stone. Through visualizing and reading the glossary, I was better able to understand the word.*

Have students take notes on other words that cause confusion. Explain that by clicking on the words in red, students can get a quick definition.

## Comprehension support

↬ *The title of this first section is A Useful Tool. Why are maps useful? Let's fill out the Making Inferences Chart. What is in the text? Let's put that in the first column.* (Maps are tools that help you find your way.) *What do we know about maps? Let's add that to the second column.* (Students might say we can use maps when we are lost.) *What inference can you make about why maps are useful?* (A map is useful because it helps people find their way when they are lost.)

↬ *This section is about symbols. Let's make an inference about why maps include symbols for real places.* (Clues in the Text: A blue line stands for a river. A triangle stands for a mountain. What I Know: Answers will vary. Students may say it's easy to read symbols on map. Inference: Maps include symbols because they are easy to read.)

↬ *What other inferences can we make as we read "What Is a Map?"* (Acknowledge and accept student responses.)

## Collaborative practice ✎

Encourage student pairs to draw a map of a place and to include the features discussed in the article: cardinal directions, symbols, and a key. Students may find it helpful to have a little more review on the parts of the map, or to read the additional items listed under **Further research**. They can also refer to the article and their Making Inferences Chart as they're working.

For further study on the topic, try the activity as a class. Click on the paper and crayon icon in the "What Is a Map?" article, find Share what you know, and click on Print.

# Where do I find landforms on a map?

## Introduce the topic

*Landforms are a natural feature of land. Can you think of any landforms near your home or near the school?* (Acknowledge and accept student responses. Consider discussing an example for students as needed.)

*Maps often show landforms. Some maps even show bumps for the different landforms. These kinds of maps are called physical maps. Today, we are going to talk about landforms and learn how to find them on maps.*

It may be helpful to review common landforms prior to showing students maps with the landforms. The following PebbleGo articles include pictures of different types of landforms: "Mountains," "Rivers," "Lakes," and "Living on the Plains."

*Today we are going to read the PebbleGo article "U.S. Landforms on Maps." To begin, let's fill in a Question Words Chart. We will use this chart to write questions we have about U.S. landforms before and as we read the article. As we read, we will write down the answers to our questions. Writing down our questions and the answers we find is a helpful way to keep track of what we learn. We can use these notes later on as we create our own maps.*

*What is on a map? Let's write this question on the chart under "What?" and then fill in the chart with our answers.* (Model for students, such as countries and bodies of water.) *What are some other questions we have about landforms on maps? Where might we get the answers to these questions?* (Acknowledge student responses, filling in the correct part of the chart.)

*As we read the PebbleGo article "U.S. Landforms on Maps," let's fill in the chart.*

Depending on the level of support needed, have students read or listen to the article, or read the article to students. The instruction that follows will help to support comprehension of the content as well as connect students to the social studies topic.

### Standards

**College and Career Readiness Standards:**
CCSS.ELA-Literacy.CCRA.R.1,
CCSS.ELA-Literacy.CCRA.R.2,
CCSS.ELA-Literacy.CCRA.R.4,
CCSS.ELA-Literacy.CCRA.L.4,
CCSS.ELA-Literacy.CCRA.L.6

**AASL Standards Framework for Learners:**
I.A.1, I.A.2, I.B.3, I.D.1, I.D.2, I.D.3, III.A.1, III.A.2, III.D.1, IV.B.1, VI.A.1

### Materials

- "U.S. Landforms on Maps" PebbleGo article
- Question Words Chart, p. 119
- Art supplies: construction paper, markers, and crayons

## Differentiation

For **Collaborative practice**, students at a lower level may have an easier time working on this assignment as a whole or small group, with outlines provided by you. Provide additional support on map features as possible, including reviewing the landforms: mountain ranges, rivers, lakes, and plains. Post student maps when completed.

### Further research

- PebbleGo "Map Symbols and Keys"
- PebbleGo "Physical Maps"
- PebbleGo "What Is a Map?"
- Besel, Jennifer M. *Types of Maps*. Maps. North Mankato, Minn.: Capstone Press, 2014.
- Brennan, Linda Crotta. *Maps: What You Need to Know*. Fact Files. North Mankato, Minn.: Capstone Press, 2018.

# Vocabulary support

Be on the lookout for vocabulary words that students do not know. Encourage students to share these words with the class. Students can use strategies, such as using picture support, in order to understand the word's meaning.

*I noticed some of you were not sure what the term "physical maps" means.* (From Landforms on Maps) *Let's take a closer look at the sentence it is in to see if there is a clue, or hint, to its meaning. The sentence says, "On physical maps of the United States, you might see the bumps of mountains, the blue line of rivers, and the flat land of plains." It seems like the author is giving us a description of what a physical map is. I could look at the picture to help me better understand what a physical map is. The picture shows all of the landforms discussed in the sentence. When I click on the term, I see that it means "a map that shows the physical features on Earth, such as mountains or lakes," and the picture does show a map with land features. Looking at the picture and reading its definition helped me figure out the meaning of an unknown phrase.*

Have students take notes on other words that cause confusion. Explain that by clicking on the words in red, students can get a quick definition.

# Comprehension support

⇨ *Why do you think mountains appear as bumps on a map?* (Students may say because the bumps are symbols for mountains.) *Let's add the question and this answer to our chart.*

⇨ *Take a look at the section called Mountains. What mountain ranges are in the United States? Let's add this question and the answer to the chart.* (The Rocky Mountains and the Appalachian Mountains) *Are there any questions you had as you read about Mountains?*

⇨ *Why are rivers an important part of a map? Where did you read this information?* (Rivers help form borders of states; Rivers section.)

⇨ *Have students review the remaining tabs, writing down their questions and answers found as they read.*

⇨ *What did we learn about U.S. landforms on maps from reading this article? What kinds of questions and answers did we add to our Question Words Chart?* (Acknowledge and accept student responses.)

# Collaborative practice ✐

During this **Collaborative practice**, students will be challenged to draw a physical map of a state or a country. Provide lots of reference materials, such as those listed under **Further research**. Students may be interested in tracing the boundary lines for the state or country and then filling it in with the land features.

For further study on the topic, try the activity as a class. Click on the paper and crayon icon in the "U.S. Landforms on Maps" article, find Share what you know, and click on Print.

# Where are cities, states, and countries on a map?

## Standards

**College and Career Readiness Standards:**
CCSS.ELA-Literacy.CCRA.R.1,
CCSS.ELA-Literacy.CCRA.R.2,
CCSS.ELA-Literacy.CCRA.R.4,
CCSS.ELA-Literacy.CCRA.L.4,
CCSS.ELA-Literacy.CCRA.L.6

**AASL Standards Framework for Learners:**
I.A.2, I.D.1, I.D.2, III.A.1,
III.A.2, III.D.1, VI.A.1

## Materials

- "Political Maps" PebbleGo article
- KWL Chart, p. 116
- Samples of political maps

## Introduce the topic

*Did you know that our state is shown on a map? Political maps have a lot of information. They show borders between states and countries. They also show cities, roads, and railroads. Why might a political map be helpful?* (Acknowledge and accept student responses.)

*I heard some of you say that political maps might be helpful to find where you are or for directions. Before people used their smartphones to get from one place to another, they used political maps.*

*Let's take a look at these political maps. What do you notice?* (Acknowledge and accept student responses.) *Let's try to find where we live. What do you notice?*

*Today we are going to read the PebbleGo article "Political Maps." We are also going to fill out a KWL Chart. In the first column, we will add what we know about political maps.* (Model for students, such as: I know I can find cities on a map.) *What are some of our wonderings about political maps? Is there anything you're not sure about that you hope to find out more? Let's put your wonderings into the What I Want to Know portion of the chart.* (Model for students, such as: I wonder how I might be able to find cities on a political map.)

*Let's take notes as we complete the article. Then we'll use our notes as we're exploring political maps.*

Depending on the level of support needed, have students read or listen to the article, or read the article to students. The instruction that follows will help to support comprehension of the content as well as connect students to the social studies topic.

**Social Studies Lessons:** Where are cities, states, and countries on a map?

89

## Differentiation

For **Collaborative practice,** encourage higher-level students to use a Venn Diagram (p. 122) to compare and contrast a political map to other kinds of maps. For students needing further support, it might be helpful to conduct the first part of the **Collaborative practice** as a group, with you modeling the activity with another student.

## Further research

- PebbleGo "Distribution Maps"

- PebbleGo "Physical Maps"

- PebbleGo "Topographic Maps"

- PebbleGo "What Is a Map?"

- Besel, Jennifer M. *Types of Maps.* Maps. North Mankato, Minn.: Capstone Press, 2014.

- Brennan, Linda Crotta. *Maps: What You Need to Know.* Fact Files. North Mankato, Minn.: Capstone Press, 2018.

## Vocabulary support

Be on the lookout for vocabulary words that students do not know. Encourage students to share these words with the class. Students can use strategies, such as the Four-Square strategy. This strategy works well by taking a piece of paper, folding it lengthwise, and then folding it again by its width. When you open up the paper, there should be four sections. In the middle of the page, where the sections intersect, students write the word. Starting clockwise, in the first section, students find a definition of the word. In the second section, students write a sentence with the word. The third section is an opportunity to write a synonym or antonym. For words that might not have a clear synonym or antonym, writing an example of the word can work instead (e.g., "flag" for "symbol"). In the last section, students can draw a picture of the word. It's recommended not to overuse this strategy, so as not to draw students away from the lesson, but it could be useful in order to deeply understand a word.

Have students take notes on other words that cause confusion. Explain that by clicking on the words in red, students can get a quick definition.

## Comprehension support

- ⮑ *Why do you think political maps show borders between states or countries?* (Students may say so it's clear where each state or country is.) *Let's add new findings to our chart.*

- ⮑ *I found the answer to one of my wonderings in the part called Symbols. Maps use symbols to show cities. What kind of symbol does a political map use for capital cities?* (A circle with a star in it)

- ⮑ Have students review the remaining tabs, adding to their chart as they read.

## Collaborative practice 🖉

Put students into pairs and provide each pair with a political map. Have one student look at the map, find a location, and ask his or her partner to find it. He or she can provide clues during this activity. Then the partner looks at the map to find that location. Encourage students to challenge each other with cities, rivers, and so forth. Students can take this practice to conduct extended research on maps, comparing and contrasting the different kinds of maps. The articles and books included in **Further research** will support this activity.

For further study on the topic, try the activity as a class. Click on the paper and crayon icon in the "Political Maps" article, find Share what you know, and click on Print.

# What is a symbol?

## Introduce the topic

*A symbol is something that stands for something else. A heart is a symbol for love. What are some symbols you know about?* (Acknowledge and accept student responses.)

*I heard some of you say that flags are a symbol for a country or a state. We see flags in many places. Where are some places you have seen flags?* (Acknowledge and accept student responses.)

*You're right! Flags can be seen all over, from outside buildings and in schools to the Olympics. The U.S. flag is a symbol for the country, but there are other symbols for the country. What are some other symbols that you know for the United States?*

*Yes, the bald eagle is a symbol for the United States of America. So is Uncle Sam. But did you know that the Pledge of Allegiance is also a symbol for the country? Today we are going to read the PebbleGo article "Pledge of Allegiance." Before, during, and after reading, we are going to fill in a Question Words Chart with questions about the Pledge of Allegiance. If the article has the answer to our question, we are going to add the answer to the chart. If not, we can do more research to find an answer. Taking notes as we read will help us further understand the text and help us in our research later on.*

*This chart includes a lot of the question words that we know: What, Who, When, Where, and Why. You might have questions that begin with How, and you can use the back of the page to include those kinds of questions. Are there any questions that you have now about the Pledge of Allegiance?* (Give students time to provide their questions. If students do not have any questions after some time, consider modeling with: "Why is the Pledge of Allegiance a symbol?")

Depending on the level of support needed, have students read or listen to the article, or read the article to students. The instruction that follows will help to support comprehension of the content as well as connect students to the social studies topic.

## Vocabulary support

Be on the lookout for vocabulary words that students do not know. The "Pledge of Allegiance" article includes some higher-level vocabulary. It may be helpful to write the words on an anchor chart and discuss students' familiarity with them. Then the anchor chart can be revisited after students read the article to discuss how well they know the words.

**College and Career Readiness Standards:**
CCSS.ELA-Literacy.CCRA.R.1,
CCSS.ELA-Literacy.CCRA.R.2,
CCSS.ELA-Literacy.CCRA.R.4,
CCSS.ELA-Literacy.CCRA.W.7,
CCSS.ELA-Literacy.CCRA.L.4,
CCSS.ELA-Literacy.CCRA.L.6

**AASL Standards Framework for Learners:**
I.A.1, I.A.2, I.B.1, I.D.1, I.D.2, III.A.1, III.A.2, III.D.1, VI.A.1

**Materials**
- "Pledge of Allegiance" PebbleGo article
- Question Words Chart, p. 119

**Further research**

- PebbleGo "American Flag"
- PebbleGo "Bald Eagle"
- PebbleGo "Star-Spangled Banner"
- PebbleGo "Uncle Sam"
- Clay, Kathryn. *The Pledge of Allegiance*. Introducing Primary Sources. North Mankato, Minn.: Capstone Press, 2016.

Sometimes adding a picture clue next to the word on the anchor chart could also help students with word recall. Choose four or five words from the article that you believe students will have trouble with in order to create the anchor chart.

As students read, also encourage them to take notes on other words that cause confusion. Explain that by clicking on the words in red, students can get a quick definition.

## Comprehension support

⮕ *Have you noticed that the titles of most sections are questions? We can add the questions to our Question Words Chart and write the answers as well. As we read we can also include our own questions.* (Consider adding the questions listed as sections in the article to the Question Words Chart.) *What did you learn about the Pledge of Allegiance in the first section?* (Acknowledge and accept student responses. They may say that it's a promise to show loyalty and respect to the United States.)

⮕ *We learned a little bit about why the Pledge of Allegiance was written in the section titled Who Wrote It? What did you learn about the author of the Pledge of Allegiance?* (Francis Bellamy wrote it because he wanted students to say it on Columbus Day.) *We don't have a lot of information about the author. Maybe we can ask the question, "Who was Francis Bellamy?" Then we can think about doing more research about him.*

⮕ *Why did the Pledge of Allegiance become a tradition in schools?* (Students and teachers liked saying it.) *Are there any questions you might have about the Pledge and traditions?* (Encourage students to think of other traditions that happen in or outside of school.)

⮕ Encourage students to read the remaining tabs and include questions (and answers) on their Question Words Chart as they read.

## Collaborative practice 🖉

During this practice, student groups may either conduct further research on the Pledge of Allegiance (using their Question Words Chart as a basis) or they can choose another symbol to read about. The goal will be for students to better understand why something is chosen as a symbol. Provide materials, such as those listed in **Further research**. Students may also research online or at the library with adult supervision. Encourage student groups to take notes and share out their findings with the wider group.

For further study on the topic, try the activity as a class. Click on the paper and crayon icon in the "Pledge of Allegiance" article, find Share what you know, and click on Print.

# Why are certain buildings important?

## Standards

**College and Career Readiness Standards:**
CCSS.ELA-Literacy.CCRA.R.1,
CCSS.ELA-Literacy.CCRA.R.2,
CCSS.ELA-Literacy.CCRA.R.4,
CCSS.ELA-Literacy.CCRA.W.7,
CCSS.ELA-Literacy.CCRA.L.4,
CCSS.ELA-Literacy.CCRA.L.6

**AASL Standards Framework for Learners:**
I.A.1, I.A.2, I.B.3, I.D.1, I.D.2, III.A.1, III.A.2, III.D.1, VI.A.1

## Materials

- "White House" PebbleGo article
- Timeline, p. 124

## Introduce the topic

*Where does the president of the United States live?* (Acknowledge student responses.)

*That's right! The president of the United States lives in the White House. He also works out of the White House. Did you know that people can tour, or visit, the White House? What makes this building so important?* (Acknowledge and accept student responses.)

*I heard some of you say it's important because that's where the president lives. But did you know it is a symbol as well? Some buildings can be symbols for something else. For example, the U.S. Supreme Court building is a symbol for justice and law because important decisions for our country are made there.*

*Today we are going to read the PebbleGo article about the White House. As we read, we are going to fill in a timeline. The earliest dates go on the left-hand side of the timeline. The later dates appear on the right-hand side. We are then going to use a fresh timeline to research another symbolic building of the United States and compare the two timelines.*

Depending on the level of support needed, have students read or listen to the article, or read the article to students. The instruction that follows will help to support comprehension of the content as well as connect students to the social studies topic.

## Vocabulary support

Be on the lookout for vocabulary words that students do not know. Encourage students to share these words with the class. Students can use strategies, such as seeking out other references, in order to understand new vocabulary.

*I noticed some of you were not sure what the word "democracy" means. (From What Is It?) Let's take a closer look at the sentence it is in to see if there is a clue, or hint, to its meaning. The sentence says, "The White House is a symbol of American democracy." After reading this sentence, I understand that the White House is a symbol, but I'm still not sure what the meaning of the word "democracy" is. Sometimes if we come across an unknown word, it's helpful to seek out another reference, like a thesaurus. By looking up the word in a thesaurus, I learn that similar words for "democracy" are "justice," "freedom," and "the American Way." I now understand that the White House is a symbol of freedom and justice. I'm also going to click on the word "democracy" because the red color lets me know the word is linked to a glossary definition. By seeing the definition, I learn that "democracy" is "a kind of government in which the people make decisions by voting." This connects to the idea of freedom and justice.*

Have students take notes on other words that cause confusion. Explain that by clicking on the words in red, students can get a quick definition.

## Comprehension support

- ▷ *How often do the American people vote for a new president? (Every four years) Where can this information be found? (What Is It?)*
- ▷ *There was a contest held to design the White House. Let's add the date and a sentence about who won the contest to our timelines. (From Who Built It? section: 1792, James Hoban's design won the contest.)*
- ▷ *When did workers begin building the White House? When was it finished? Let's add this information to our timelines. (1792, Workers began building the White House; 1800, It was completed.)*
- ▷ *The White House is pretty big. Why do you think that is? (Students may say that it needs to be large for the number of guests that visit it.)*
- ▷ Encourage students to read the remaining tabs, adding information to their timeline as they read.

## Collaborative practice ✐

Provide a fresh timeline to student pairs, and encourage them to read about another important U.S. building. Students can utilize the articles in PebbleGo, or conduct their own research in the library. Have student pairs compare the timeline of the White House to the building they researched and note similarities. Also encourage students to discuss why the building they researched is important.

For further study on the topic, try the activity as a class. Click on the paper and crayon icon in the "White House" article, find Share what you know, and click on Print.

# Comprehension Lessons

# Using prior knowledge

When students consider what they already know about the topic, they gain a deeper understanding of the text. This lesson provides support in using prior knowledge.

## Introduce the strategy

*Before we read, we think to ourselves, "What is this text about? What do we already know about it?" When we think about what we already know, it helps us understand the text better. Today, we will be using prior knowledge to better understand the PebbleGo article "Cats."*

## Model

*When we think about what we already know, we are using prior knowledge. Let's take a closer look at the article. This article is about cats, and there is a different tab for the different kinds of information we will learn about cats. The first tab is about the cat's body. I have seen a cat and know a cat is a small pet that has four legs and is covered with fur. I wonder what else I will learn. As I read the article, I will think about what I already know about cats. This is my prior knowledge, and it will help me understand what I read.*

## Guided practice

➪ *Turn and talk to a partner. Explain how what you know about cats might help you understand what you read about cats.*

➪ Encourage student responses. Guide students as needed in order to have the direction of the discussion turn to what students know about cats and how that knowledge might help them understand the article. *I heard some of you talking about how what you already know about cats will help you understand where cats live and what they look like.*

➪ *How might what you know about nonfiction help you read the article? Turn and talk with a partner.*

➪ Encourage student responses. Guide students as needed to talk about the text features in nonfiction that will support comprehension. *I heard some of you talk about how you know to use pictures to give you more information on the topic. How are nonfiction articles organized? How might this organization help you as you read?* (Acknowledge and accept student responses.)

# Collaborative practice

Have students work in small groups with the following questions and share their responses with the whole group.

- ➪ *Take a look at the first section on cat bodies. What does this topic make you think of? Does anyone have a cat as a pet? What is its body like?*

- ➪ *Now read the text. Is there anything new that you learned? Talk with your group.*

- ➪ *The next section is about a cat's habitat. Can anyone explain what a habitat is? How might the picture help you understand this word?* (Encourage students to share their answers. As needed, help guide the conversation about habitats, explaining that a habitat is the place where an animal, plant, or other living thing lives. Encourage students to connect the picture to the definition.)

- ➪ *Now read the text. What did you already know about a cat's habitat? What did you learn?*

- ➪ *Let's think about the types of food that cats eat. What do you already know about a cat's diet?* (Encourage students to share their responses.)

- ➪ *Now read the text. Was there any information that seemed to be missing from the article?*

# Independent work ✐

Have students practice using their prior knowledge independently with the remaining tabs. Provide a copy of the T-Chart for each student.

*We are going to use a T-Chart to take notes as we read. We will write down a title for the first column of the chart. Let's write the title What I Know for this side. Now let's come up with a title for the second column. Let's call it What I Learned. As we read the rest of the article, I will ask you questions. You will write your responses on the T-Chart.*

- ➪ *Think about the title Life Cycle. What do you already know about life cycles? Write your answers in the first column of the chart, under What I Know.*

- ➪ *Now read (or listen to) the article. What did you learn about life cycles? Write what you learned on the side of the chart with the title What I Learned.*

- ➪ Go over the remaining tab, Fun Facts, following the example above.

- ➪ *Let's talk about some of the things you already know and some of the things you learned.* Encourage student discussion, acknowledging and accepting student responses.

# Extend the learning

Encourage further discussion about the strategy.

- ➪ *How could you use what you already know when reading nonfiction?*

- ➪ *How does using what you already know help you understand what you read?*

- ➪ *Think about the steps you go through to complete a science experiment. How might using what you know help you as you're doing a science experiment?*

- ➪ Encourage students to practice the strategy with one of the related articles, "About Mammals" or "Ferrets."

## Standards

**College and Career Readiness Standards:**
CCSS.ELA-Literacy.CCRA.R.1,
CCSS.ELA-Literacy.CCRA.R.2

**AASL Standards Framework for Learners:**
I.A.2, I.D.1, III.A.2, III.D.1,
VI.A.1

## Materials

- "People in Spring" PebbleGo article
- Making Connections Chart, p. 118

# Making connections

As readers, we connect texts we are reading to our own experiences, other texts, or what we know about the world. Tapping into those connections allows deeper thinking about the text and understandings about content, both in informational and fictional text. This lesson will provide the opportunity to practice making connections with informational text.

## Introduce the strategy

*Sometimes when I read, I think to myself "This reminds me of another book I read," or "This reminds me of something that happened to me." That's called making connections. We can connect the text to another text we read; our experiences, such as something we saw; or to our world. Let's take a few moments to talk about how each of those connections might be different.* (Direct conversation to how the types of connections are different. For example, something we read is different from something we might see in our community. It's also different from something we might see on the news.) *Today, we will be making connections to better understand the PebbleGo article "People in Spring."*

## Model

*We are making connections when we link the text to another text, to ourselves, or to the world around us. Let's take a closer look at the article. This article is about spring.* (Read aloud to students the first tab labeled What Is Spring?) *I read, "People enjoy being outdoors after the long, cold winter." From my own experience, I know that when the weather becomes warmer, I like to be outside more. I connected the text to myself to better understand spring weather. As we read, let's continue to make connections to better understand what we read.*

## Guided practice

⮕ *Turn and talk to a partner. Explain how making connections might help you understand what you read about spring weather.*

⮕ Encourage student responses. Guide students as needed in order to have the direction of the discussion turn to what students know about spring weather. If you live in a climate that doesn't experience a warm springtime after a harsh winter, guide the conversation to text-to-world connections, such as stories heard on the news, or text-to-text connections, like books read on the subject.

- *I heard some of you talking about how making connections will help you understand that people might enjoy spring after experiencing a very cold and snowy winter.*
- *Let's take a look the first section, What Is Spring? Let's read it together and talk about some additional connections we can make to the text, such as text-to-self and text-to-text connections.*
- Encourage student responses. *I heard some of you talk about your own feelings about spring. Keep thinking about text-to-self, text-to-text, and text-to-world connections as we read the text.*

## Collaborative practice

Have students work in small groups with the following questions and share their responses with the whole group.

- *Take a look at the first section called What Is Spring? Have you read any books or website articles about this topic?*
- *Now read the text. Talk with your group about how this article is similar to or different from other texts you read about the subject.*
- *The next section is called What to Wear. Take a look at the picture. Have you ever experienced what this girl is experiencing?*
- *Now read the text. Talk with your group about some of the clothes you have worn during spring weather.*
- *Let's think about the next section, Spring Sports. What kinds of sports do people play during the spring? Where have you seen people play these sports? (Encourage students to share their responses.)*
- *Now read the text. Were there some sports listed that you haven't thought about? Was there any information that seemed to be missing from the article? Think about some of the sports you may have seen on TV in order to answer this question.*

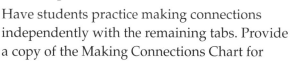

## Independent work

Have students practice making connections independently with the remaining tabs. Provide a copy of the Making Connections Chart for each student.

*We are going to use the Making Connections Chart to take notes as we read. As we read the rest of the article, I will ask you questions. You will write your responses in the chart. In the first column, you will write the part of the text that you had made a connection to. In the second column, you will write about your connection and whether the connection is to another text, to the world, or to yourself.*

- *Read (or listen to) the part of the article labeled Spring Work. What kinds of connections did you make to the text? Write down your responses in the chart. Did you learn anything new?* (Take note of student responses to share during **Extend the learning**.)
- Go over the remaining tab, Spring Food, following the example above.
- *Let's talk about some of the connections that you made.* Encourage student discussion, acknowledging and accepting student responses.

## Extend the learning

Encourage further discussion about the strategy.

- *How did making connections help you as you read this article? Was any information new to you?*
- *Was it easier to come up with connections to yourself? What kinds of connections were most difficult to make? Why do you think that is?*
- *Was there text that you were not clear about? Let's share that as a group. Perhaps someone else was able to make a connection that will help clarify the text.*
- Encourage students to practice the strategy with other articles about spring: "Spring Weather," "Animals in Spring," "Flower Blossoms," or "Plants in Spring."

**Standards**

**College and Career Readiness Standards:**
CCSS.ELA-Literacy.CCRA.R.1,
CCSS.ELA-Literacy.CCRA.R.2

**AASL Standards Framework for Learners:**
I.A.2, I.D.1, III.A.2, III.D.1, VI.A.1

**Materials**

- "Volcanoes" PebbleGo article
- T-Chart, p. 117

# Making predictions

Readers make predictions before, during, and even after they read. Before they read, readers look at the table of contents, pictures, and other text features, such as highlighted or boldfaced vocabulary, to make predictions about what they will read. As they're reading, readers make predictions about what will happen next. After reading, readers sometimes think about how the text could be extended, and they make predictions about what that information could be about. This lesson will provide the opportunity to practice making predictions with informational text.

## Introduce the strategy

*If I see a text that begins with, "Once upon a time," I know it will be fiction. If I see lots of photographs or titles or subheads for parts of text, I know the text will be nonfiction. I can use my knowledge of fiction and nonfiction texts to help me predict what those texts will be about. Today, we will be making predictions to better understand the PebbleGo article "Volcanoes."*

## Model

*When we figure out what is happening next, we are predicting. Let's take a closer look at the article. This article is about volcanoes. The tabs at the top tell me what I will read about. The different parts of the article are: What Are They? What Causes Them?, Volcano Damage, Where Are They?, and Studying Volcanoes. From looking at the topics, I predict I am going to learn a lot of different information about volcanoes. In What Are They?, I predict I am going to read about the definition of a volcano. I am going to read the text to find out if I am correct.* (Read the text out loud.) *I predicted correctly! A volcano is an opening in Earth's surface that sends hot lava, rocks, and gas into the air.* (This segment has a lot of academic vocabulary. Take time as needed to review the vocabulary to support comprehension.) *As we read, let's continue to make predictions to better understand what we read.*

## Guided practice

⇨ *Turn and talk to a partner. Explain how making predictions might help you understand what you read about volcanoes.*

⇨ Encourage student responses. Guide students as needed in order to have the direction of the discussion turn to the parts of the article.

➪ *I heard some of you talking about how using the titles for each tab will help you predict what you will read about. Someone had mentioned that they hope to learn more about what happens beneath the earth's surface in What Causes Them? Let's see if that prediction will be helpful as we read the text.*

➪ *Let's take a look the first tab, What Are They? Let's take a closer look at the picture. How does the picture help you in making predictions about what you will read? What makes you think of this? Now read the text. How did the picture support your understanding of the text?*

➪ Encourage student responses. *I heard some of you talk about how the picture shows a volcano with steam coming out of it. In reading the text, some of you mentioned that you weren't sure what "erupts" means but the picture had helped. Keep making these predictions as we read the text.*

## Collaborative practice

Have students work in small groups with the following questions and share their responses with the whole group.

➪ *Take a look at the second tab called What Causes Them? After reading the title, what do you think the text might be about? Why do you think that?* (Acknowledge and accept student responses.)

➪ *Now read the text. Were your predictions correct? Were there other features you used to make a prediction?* (This section includes some academic vocabulary terms. As needed, review the terms prior to discussing the text. Students may say they used the vocabulary to make predictions.)

➪ *The next tab is called Volcano Damage. Take a look at the picture. How does the picture help you make a prediction about the text?*

➪ *Now read the text. What types of damage happen after a volcano erupts? Were you able to make predictions about the damage?* (Encourage students to share their responses.)

## Independent work ✏

Have students practice making connections independently with the remaining tabs. Provide a copy of the T-Chart for each student.

*We are going to use a T-Chart to take notes as we read. We will write down a title for the first side of the chart. Let's write the title Predictions for this side. Now let's come up with a title for the second side of the chart. Let's call it What I Learned. As we read the rest of the article, I will ask you questions. You will write your responses on the T-Chart.*

➪ *Look at the part of the article labeled Where Are They? What kinds of predictions can you make about what you will read? Write down your responses on the first side of the chart labeled Predictions. What did you use to make a prediction? Write that down in the chart.*

➪ *Now read the text. Did your predictions help you? What new information did you learn? Add that to the second side of the chart.*

➪ Go over the remaining tab, Studying Volcanoes, following the example above.

➪ *Let's talk about some of the predictions that you had made. What did you use to make these predictions?* Encourage student discussion, acknowledging and accepting student responses.

## Extend the learning

Encourage further discussion about the strategy.

➪ *How did making predictions help you as you read this article?*

➪ *Take a look at the part of the article labeled Studying Volcanoes. It says, "Scientists try to predict when a volcano will erupt." The word "predict" is in this part of the article. How is a scientist's prediction like making predictions when we read? How might it be different?*

➪ *Was there text that you were not clear about? Let's share that as a group.* (This article has many academic vocabulary words, and students may benefit from a discussion about them. Encourage students to discuss the terms that are unfamiliar to them.)

➪ Encourage students to practice the strategy with other articles from the Earth in Action category: "Avalanches," "Earthquakes," "Floods," "Tsunamis," or "Wildfires."

## Standards

**College and Career Readiness Standards:**
CCSS.ELA-Literacy.CCRA.R.1,
CCSS.ELA-Literacy.CCRA.R.2

**AASL Standards Framework for Learners:**
I.A.2, I.D.1, III.A.2, III.D.1, VI.A.1

## Materials

- "Firefighters" PebbleGo article
- Copies of the last two pages of "Firefighters" PebbleGo article
- Highlighters

Strategic readers continually think about their reading. When readers ask themselves, "Does this make sense?" during and after reading, they increase their understanding of the text and the vocabulary. This lesson will provide the opportunity to practice monitoring reading with informational text.

## Introduce the strategy

*Sometimes when we read, we might come across words or ideas we don't understand. If something doesn't make sense, what can we do?* (Acknowledge and accept student responses.)

## Model

*I heard some of you say that when we don't understand what we are reading, we can reread what we read. That is one way to monitor our reading. We can also slow down, sound out words, or even look to other resources, such as the glossary, to help us. Today, we will be monitoring our reading to better understand the PebbleGo article "Firefighters." Let's take a closer look at the article. I am going to start by reading the first part that is called Firefighters.* (Read the text out loud, and stumble over the word "disaster.") *I am not sure how to read this word, so I am going to break it down by its syllables* (write the word on the board, and place a backslash after each syllable. Read each syllable slowly, and then read the word as a whole): *di/sas/ter, disaster. Notice how I sounded out each syllable slowly in order to understand what I read. I'm still not sure I know the meaning of "disaster," but I see that the word is red. I can click on the word for a definition. Now I understand that firefighters are there to help with disasters, which are events that cause a lot of damage. I'm so glad firefighters are there to help us. As we read, let's continue to monitor to better understand what we read.*

## Guided practice

➪ *Turn and talk to a partner. Explain how monitoring might help you understand what you read about firefighters.*

➪ Encourage student responses. Guide students as needed in order to have the direction of the discussion turn to ways to monitor reading: slowing down, rereading the text, and sounding out a word. Other suggestions include looking for context clues or looking up words in a dictionary or glossary.

➪ *Let's take a look the first tab, Firefighters. Try reading* (or listening) *to the text on your own.* (Wait a few moments for students to read the text.) *Were there parts of the text you needed some help with? What were those parts? Were there any strategies you used to help you better understand what you read?*

➪ Encourage student responses. *I heard some of you talk about how the first sentence was unclear to you because you were not sure what the word "trained" meant. Some of you looked up the word in the dictionary. Another asked a friend to work out the meaning of the sentence. How did this sentence help you better understand the article? Keep monitoring as we read the text.*

## Collaborative practice

Have students work in small groups with the following questions and share their responses with the whole group.

➪ *Take a look at the part of the article called What Firefighters Do. Read the text.*

➪ *Did you understand everything you read? Which parts of the text were unclear?* (Acknowledge and accept student responses.) *Try removing the word that is unclear. Did the sentence make sense? Were there other words near that word that helped you figure out the meaning?* (Allow for students to share their strategy use with the group.) *Sometimes it's helpful to use context clues, or clues around the word, to help us figure out the meaning of an unknown word.*

➪ *The next part is called Clothes. Now read the text.*

➪ *Were there any parts or words that seemed unclear to you? How did you figure out what sounded correct?* (Encourage students to share their responses.)

# Independent work

Have students practice monitoring what they read independently with the remaining tabs. Provide a copy of the last two pages of the article and a highlighter to each student.

*We are going to use a copy of the article and a highlighter. As we read the rest of the article, highlight any words or phrases that are unclear to you. Take note of some of the strategies you used to understand those words.*

➪ *Look at the part of the article labeled Tools. Read the text beneath the title. Highlight any words or phrases that you do not understand.*

➪ *Take a look at the words you highlighted. What do you think would make sense? Are there other words around or near this word that might help you figure out what it means?*

➪ Go over the remaining tab, Fire Trucks, following the example above.

➪ *Let's talk about some of words or phrases that you highlighted. What strategies did you use to correct your reading?* Encourage student discussion, acknowledging and accepting student responses. Encourage students to look at the Glossary Terms section for support.

## Extend the learning

Encourage further discussion about the strategy.

➪ *How did monitoring help you read this article?*

➪ *Were there any words for which you came up with a synonym, or a similar word, in order to understand the text?*

➪ *Was there text that you were not clear about? Let's share that as a group.* (This article has some academic vocabulary words, and students may benefit from a discussion about them.)

➪ Encourage students to practice the strategy with other articles from the Jobs in the Community category: "Veterinarians," "Police Officers," "Farmers," and so on.

## Standards

**College and Career Readiness Standards:**
CCSS.ELA-Literacy.CCRA.R.1,
CCSS.ELA-Literacy.CCRA.R.2

**AASL Standards Framework for Learners:**
I.A.2, I.D.1, III.A.2, III.D.1, VI.A.1

## Materials

• "Martin Luther King Jr." PebbleGo article

• Question Words Chart, p. 119

Strategic readers ask questions before, during, and after they read. Before reading, their questions can guide their navigation of the text. While they read, they ask questions that are raised by the text and seek answers. After reading, they may have more questions. Questions may be literal, inferential, or evaluative. While the teacher often asks questions, strategic readers ask questions and use the text to find evidence that supports their answers.

## Introduce the strategy

*Questions guide us as we read. Before we read a text, we can take a look at the topic, the cover, the title, and the pictures. That might make us wonder about the text. When we ask questions, we'll look for answers as we read. When we read, we might have even more questions. And after reading, there may still be things we wonder. As we ask questions, we can look for evidence, or proof, in the text to help us answer them. Some questions might be answered simply by looking at the text. For some questions, we need to think not only about the text, but also what we know from our own lives and experiences. Today, we will be questioning as we read to better understand the PebbleGo article "Martin Luther King Jr."*

## Model

*This article is about Martin Luther King Jr. I am going to start by reading the first part that is called Introduction. (Read the text out loud.) The text says that in 1929, ". . . whites and people of color were segregated." My question is: What does "segregated" mean? By rereading the sentence, I know it has to do with people who are white and people who are of color. I see that the word is in red, so I can click on it to find out the answer to my question. I learned "segregated" means to be "divided by skin color." Now I understand what the word means and why Martin's father would want him to demand respect.*

## Guided practice

⟳ *Turn and talk to a partner. Explain how questioning might help you understand a nonfiction text. How do you think you can find the answers to your questions?*

⟳ Encourage student responses. Guide students as needed in order to have the direction of the discussion turn to places to go for information. The answers sometimes appear in the text. Also talk about if students have questions that the text does not answer. Sometimes students will be using what they know from their own experiences and background knowledge to answer the questions. They can also go to other resources, such as books on the topic, for guidance.

⮑ *Let's think about some question words we can ask as we read. What are some of those question words?* (Guide a discussion about the question words: What, Who, When, Where, and Why. Sample questions include: What does that word mean? Who took action? Why did that happen? When did this happen? Consider writing them on chart paper for students to use as a reference.)

# Collaborative practice

Have students work in small groups with the following questions and share their responses with the whole group.

⮑ *Let's take a look at the part called Introduction. Are there any questions you have as you read? What seemed unclear to you?* (Encourage students to share their questions and to discuss them with the group.)

⮑ *The next part is called Education. Let's read the text.*

⮑ *Were there any parts or words that seemed unclear to you? What questions could you ask, and where can you go to get the answers? If you did not find the answer in the text, do you think the next few parts will include the answer?* (Acknowledge and accept student responses. A student may have the answer to another student's question. Allow discussion to unfold.)

# Independent work ✎

Have students practice questioning what they read independently with the remaining tabs.

*We are going to use a Question Words Chart to take notes as we read. As you read, write your question in the correct place. If your question begins with "What," write your question in the "What" box and so on. If you can find the answer to your question, also write the answer in the box.*

⮑ *Read (or listen to) the section of the article called "Life's Work." Do you have any questions about this section? Write them down on the chart.*

⮑ *Take a look at the questions that you wrote. Where do you think you can find the answers? Is it something that you might already know about, or might the answers be in the text? If you found an answer, write it down in the chart.*

⮑ Go over the remaining tabs, Last Years and Contributions, following the previous example.

⮑ *Let's talk about some of the questions that you asked. What strategies did you use to find the answers?* Encourage student discussion, acknowledging and accepting student responses.

# Extend the learning

Encourage further discussion about the strategy.

⮑ *How did questioning help you as you read this article?*

⮑ *Where did you find most of the answers to your questions?*

⮑ *Were there questions you were unable to answer? Let's share those questions as a group.* (Allow students time to share their questions and discuss where they might be able to go for the answers. Encourage them to choose one question to research.)

⮑ Encourage students to practice the strategy with other articles in the Related Articles section: "Dolores Huerta" and "Nelson Mandela."

# Visualizing

## Standards

**College and Career Readiness Standards:**
CCSS.ELA-Literacy.CCRA.R.1,
CCSS.ELA-Literacy.CCRA.R.2

**AASL Standards Framework for Learners:**
I.A.2, I.D.1, III.A.2, III.D.1, VI.A.1

## Materials

- "Chinese New Year" PebbleGo article
- T-Chart, p. 117

Strategic readers consider sensory images, looking for words that evoke the senses of sight, sound, smell, taste, and touch. These sensory images allow for deeper understanding of the content and give readers a "you are there" feeling as they read.

## Introduce the strategy

*Imagine that you are reading about a cold winter day. You might read about the sight of trees and houses covered in snow, the feel of the cold, the sound of the wind blowing against the windows of a house, and the smell of hot chocolate. When we visualize what we read, we try to see, smell, taste, touch, and hear what is happening. Visualizing, or picturing, what we read helps us to better understand it. Today we will be visualizing what we read to better understand the PebbleGo article "Chinese New Year."*

## Model

*As I'm reading today, I'll think about my senses and use them to visualize the text. I am going to read the section of the article that begins with "Chinese New Year." (Read the text aloud.) There are not many describing words in the article, but I can use some of the text to picture what is going on. The text says, "Chinese New Year is celebrated between January 21 and February 19 in China." I can picture the months in my mind, and I can call to mind the kinds of things that happen in a celebration. As we read today, be on the lookout for words that help you picture things you can see, touch, taste, smell, and hear.*

## Guided practice

- *Turn and talk to a partner. Explain how visualizing might help you understand what you read about Chinese New Year.*

- Encourage student responses. Guide students to think about the kinds of words that will help them visualize what they will read.

- *Let's take a look the second section, A Monster Legend. Try reading (or listening) to the text on your own.* (Wait a few moments for students to read the text.) *Were there parts of the text you were able to visualize? What words did you use to picture the text in your mind?*

- Encourage student responses. *I heard some of you talk about how the monster was afraid of certain things, like lights, noise, and the color red. Many mentioned they could see in their mind a monster afraid of these things. Good job using visualizing to understand what you read! Let's continue using this strategy as we read more of the article.*

# Collaborative practice

Have students work in small groups with the following questions and share their responses with the whole group.

- ⤷ *Take a look at the section titled Getting Ready. Read the text.*

- ⤷ *Could you picture what you read using the details from the text? What were you able to see? (Acknowledge and accept student responses.)*

- ⤷ *We used our sense of sight to picture the text. Were there other senses you could use? How about your sense of hearing? What words helped you hear what was going on in the text? How about touch?*

- ⤷ *Were there any parts or words that seemed unclear to you? How can you use visualizing to clarify what you read? (Encourage students to share their responses.)*

# Independent work ✎

Have students practice visualizing what they read independently with the remaining tabs.

*We are going to use a T-Chart to take notes as we read. We will write down a title for the first side of the chart. Let's write the title Our Senses for this side. Now let's come up with a title for the second side of the chart. Let's call it Information from the Text. As we read the rest of the article, I will ask you questions. In the first side of the T-Chart, you will write the sense you used to picture what you are reading.* (It may be helpful to write the following words on the board for students to reference: seeing, hearing, tasting, touching, smelling.) *In the second side, you will write down the words from the text that made you think of this sense.*

- ⤷ *Look at the part of the article labeled New Year's Eve. Read the text beneath the title and look for words or phrases that help you visualize the text.*

- ⤷ *Write the sense you could use to visualize the text. Then write the words from the text.*

- ⤷ *Go over the remaining tab, New Year's Day, following the previous example.*

- ⤷ *Let's talk about some of words or phrases that you wrote down. How did visualizing help you better understand the text?* Encourage student discussion, acknowledging and accepting student responses.

# Extend the learning

Encourage further discussion about the strategy.

- ⤷ *How did visualizing help you as you read this article?*

- ⤷ *Were there parts of the text for which you'd like to see more explanation? Which parts were those? How do you think the text could be changed to include some details?*

- ⤷ *Was there text that you were not clear about? Let's share that part as a group.* (This article has some academic vocabulary words, and students may benefit from a discussion about the terms.)

- ⤷ Encourage students to practice the strategy with other articles in the Related Articles section: "Diwali" and "Kwanzaa."

# Inferring

## Standards

**College and Career Readiness Standards:**
CCSS.ELA-Literacy.CCRA.R.1,
CCSS.ELA-Literacy.CCRA.R.2

**AASL Standards Framework for Learners:**
I.A.2, I.D.1, III.A.2, III.D.1, VI.A.1

## Materials

- "Bald Eagle" PebbleGo article
- Making Inferences Chart, p. 120

An inference is like a guess in that the reader thinks beyond the literal words on the page. Unlike a guess, an inference is based on evidence from the text and what the reader already knows about the topic.

## Introduce the strategy

*Using information in the text to figure out something is called "inferring." When I read the text, I think about the clues in the text and my own experiences to make an inference. Today we will be making inferences as we read to better understand the PebbleGo article "Bald Eagle."*

## Model

*I am going to read the section of the article that begins with "What Is It?"* (Read the text aloud.) *When I started reading the text, I noticed that the text says "The bald eagle is a national symbol of the United States." I know that a symbol is an object that stands for something else, and I've seen other national symbols like the U.S. flag and the Statue of Liberty. From what I've read about symbols, I know they are important. I can make an inference that the bald eagle must be important to the nation because it is a national symbol.*

## Guided practice

▷ *Turn and talk to a partner. Explain how making inferences might help you understand what you read about the bald eagle.*

▷ Encourage student responses. Guide students to think about how details from the text along with experiences help make for great inferences.

▷ *Let's take a look the second section called What Does It Mean? Try reading (or listening) to the text on your own.* (Wait a few moments for students to read the text.) *Let's work together to come up with an inference on why the bald eagle may have been chosen as a symbol of freedom. What do we know about freedom?* (Encourage student responses.) *How does the bald eagle stand for freedom?* (Encourage student responses.) *What does the text say about freedom?*

▷ *I heard someone talk about how a bald eagle flies, so it seems to be free. Then that person said that the American colonists had to fight for their freedom, so they made an inference that the bald eagle is a good symbol for freedom.*

# Collaborative practice

Have students work in small groups with the following questions and share their responses with the whole group.

  ⟶ *Take a look at the next section titled Who Chose It? Read the text.*

  ⟶ *What can you infer about why Congress put the picture of the bald eagle on the Great Seal?* (Acknowledge and accept student responses.)

  ⟶ Encourage student responses. Students might say that Congress really liked the picture and they wanted to do something important with it. Have students share personal experiences that might be similar. For example, students might like a certain character they see on TV or at the movies, so they might own something with that character on it.

# Independent work ✎

Have students practice making inferences on what they read independently with the remaining tabs.

*We are going to use a Making Inferences Chart to take notes as we read. I will ask you questions as we read today. In the first column, you will write down clues from the text. In the second column, you will write about what you know about that topic. Then you'll use both of those pieces of information to make an inference.*

  ⟶ *Look at the part of the article labeled History. Read the text.*

  ⟶ *Look at the first sentence. Can you make an inference about why bald eagles nearly died out? What does the text say? What do you know about DDT? Fill in the chart with these details and your inference.* (Allow time for students to work through their inferences.)

  ⟶ Go over the remaining tab, Where to See It, following the example above. To support making inferences, you could talk about how important the bald eagle has become.

  ⟶ *Let's talk about some of the information you wrote down.* Encourage student discussion, acknowledging and accepting student responses.

# Extend the learning

Encourage further discussion about the strategy.

  ⟶ *How did making inferences help you as you read this article?*

  ⟶ *Were there parts for which it was difficult to make an inference? Why do you think it was difficult?*

  ⟶ *Were you able to use your own experiences to make an inference? How did that support you as you read the text?*

  ⟶ Encourage students to practice the strategy with other articles in the Related Articles section: "Great Seal" and "Uncle Sam."

# Summarizing

## Standards

**College and Career Readiness Standards:**
CCSS.ELA-Literacy.CCRA.R.1,
CCSS.ELA-Literacy.CCRA.R.2

**AASL Standards Framework for Learners:**
I.A.2, I.D.1, III.A.2, III.D.1, VI.A.1

## Materials

- "Tornadoes" PebbleGo article
- Main Idea and Details Sheet, p. 121

When readers summarize, they demonstrate their understanding of a text by identifying key elements and then stating those important ideas in their own words.

## Introduce the strategy

*When a friend asks me to tell her about a movie, I don't tell her every single detail from the beginning to the end. I tell her only the most important things that happened. Those important ideas are a summary. Today we will be learning to summarize what we read to better understand the PebbleGo article "Tornadoes."*

## Model

*I am going to read aloud the first part of the article, What Are They?* (Read the text aloud.) *To summarize the text, I think to myself, "What are the most important parts to remember about this text?" It's not important to tell all the smaller details about what a tornado is, such as where the storm comes from. Listen to my summary. Notice how I am giving the summary in my own words: "A tornado is shaped like a funnel and travels on the ground." What do you think of my summary?* (Consider capturing these comments on a whiteboard. Note that this activity can be adjusted, but to leave out an important detail.)

*I heard some of you say that I missed an important part of the summary. I did not explain that the funnel is made of strong winds. That was great thinking! It's important not to leave out necessary details.*

## Guided practice

⇨ *Turn and talk to a partner. Explain the parts needed in a good summary.*

⇨ Encourage student responses. Guide students to think about details that are important to the main idea. It may be helpful to guide students in a discussion about the topic sentence as a good place to look to for the main idea of a paragraph. This works well with paragraphs that include the main idea in the first sentence. As texts become more complex, where the topic sentence appears varies.

⇨ *Let's take a look at the next section, How Do They Happen? Read (or listen) to the text in order to come up with a summary.* (Wait a few moments for students to read the text.) *Which parts of the text were most important? What details will need to be included in the summary?*

- Encourage student responses. *I heard some of you say that the time of year is an important part.*

- *Now let's come up with a summary.* (Provide support to the group as they are developing a summary for this segment of the text. A sample summary is: When warm air and cold air meet, usually during spring and summer, it causes wind that can form into a tornado.)

## Collaborative practice

Have students work in small groups with the following questions and share their responses with the whole group.

- *Take a look at the part titled Where Do They Happen? Read the text.*

- *What do you think the author wants us to remember? How might you be able to summarize this information?* (Acknowledge and accept student responses.)

- Support students as needed in forming a summary of this information. In this section, the first sentence is just part of the main idea. The author wants us to know that while tornadoes form all over the world, there is a part of the United States where tornadoes are very common. Guide students to create a summary based on this information.

- *Were there any parts that seemed unclear to you? How can you use summarizing to better understand what you read?* (Encourage students to share their responses.)

## Independent work ✐

Have students practice summarizing what they read independently with the remaining tabs.

Give students two copies of the Main Idea and Details Sheet. Or students can use one sheet, labeling the boxes with the part they read. *We are going to use a Main Idea and Details Sheet to take notes as we read. As we read the rest of the article, I will ask you questions. In the top box, you will write the main ideas for the text. In the bottom part, you will write the details. We will use this information to create a summary for the text.*

- *Look at the part of the article labeled What Do They Do? Read the text beneath the title.*

- *Write the main idea in your own words in the box labeled Main Idea. Then write the details that help support the main idea.* (Consider modeling these two steps for students with one of the previous sections. Then, give students a few moments to read the text and to take their notes.)

- *What did you write as the main idea?* (Guide students to understand that the main idea is tornadoes cause a lot of damage.)

- *What did you write down as the details to this text?* (Students will likely respond uprooting trees, pulling off roofs, and blowing around cars and trucks.)

- *Now think about the main idea and details that you wrote down. How can we use that information to create a summary?* (Provide assistance as needed. Summaries should include the information noted above: Tornadoes cause a lot of damage. They can uproot trees, pull off roofs, and blow around cars.)

- Go over the remaining tab, Tornado Safety, following the example above.

- *Let's talk about some of words or phrases that you wrote down. How did this information help you summarize the text?* Encourage student discussion, acknowledging and accepting student responses.

## Extend the learning

Encourage further discussion about the strategy.

- *How did summarizing help you as you read.*

- *Were you able to find the most important information? Were you able to change the text into your own words?*

- Encourage students to come up with a summary for the entire text. They may want to reread the text, noting the main idea and details as they have done during **Independent work**.

- Encourage students to practice the strategy with other articles in the Extreme Weather category: "Blizzards," "Drought," "Hurricanes," and so on.

## Standards

**College and Career Readiness Standards:**
CCSS.ELA-Literacy.CCRA.R.1,
CCSS.ELA-Literacy.CCRA.R.2

**AASL Standards Framework for Learners:**
I.A.2, I.D.1, III.A.2, III.D.1, VI.A.1

## Materials

- "Tyrannosaurus Rex" PebbleGo article
- T-Chart, p. 117

# Evaluating

S trategic readers evaluate, or make judgments about, ideas presented in text and the author's craft. Strong evaluations are supported with evidence.

## Introduce the strategy

*Sometimes when I am reading a text, I think to myself, "I really like this story!" or "I like the way the author used such great words to describe the characters." or "I didn't understand this topic very well before, but the author figured out a good way to explain things, so now I understand it." When I do this, I am evaluating what I read. Evaluating is about telling whether or not we like something. A strong evaluation has reasons. We don't just say, "I like this text." We also tell why we like the text. Similarly, we can say that we didn't like the text and give reasons for that evaluation. For example, we could explain how the text could be better. Today we will be learning to evaluate what we read to better understand the PebbleGo article "Tyrannosaurus Rex."*

## Model

*I am going to read aloud the first part of the article, Body. (Read the text aloud.) When I first read this title, I thought to myself that I am going to learn a lot about a Tyrannosaurus rex's body. I don't know too much about its body other than it was very large. Then I read on and learned quite a bit of information about the Tyrannosaurus rex. I learned just how tall it was and other information about its body. The description and the picture helped explain its body. I think the author did a good job of explaining this information, and I could give specific reasons, such as the author didn't just focus on its size but all of the dinosaur's parts.*

## Guided practice

⇨ *Turn and talk to a partner. Do you agree with me? Explain why you do or do not.*

⇨ Encourage student responses. Guide students to think about details that helped them come up with their evaluations. If they didn't like the text, encourage them to explain why.

⇨ *Let's take a look at the part called Habitat. Read (or listen) to the text in order to evaluate it. (Wait a few moments for students to read the text.) Tell me what you think is the most important information in this section? Do you think the author did a good job of explaining the text? Explain why or why not.*

⇨ Encourage student responses. *I heard some of you say that the most important part of the text is where the dinosaur could be found, and the author did a good job of explaining that.*

A Year of PebbleGo®: Connecting Content to Literacy

# Collaborative practice

Have students work in small groups with the following questions and share their responses with the whole group.

↪ *Take a look at the part titled Food. Read the text.*

↪ *What do you think the author wants us to remember? Do you think the text did a good job of explaining this information? Why or why not? (Acknowledge and accept student responses.)*

↪ Support students as needed in forming an evaluation of this section. It may be necessary to go over some of the academic vocabulary terms so students can better understand the text. Encourage students to click on the red text in order to see or hear a definition of the word.

↪ *Were there any parts that seemed unclear to you? How can you use the strategy of evaluating text to better understand what you read? (Encourage students to share their responses.)*

# Independent work ✎

Have students practice evaluating what they read independently with the remaining tabs.

*We are going to use a T-Chart to take notes as we read. We will write down a title for the first side of the chart. Let's write down What's Great! Then we'll come up with a title for the second side of the chart. Let's call it What Could Be Better. As we read the rest of the article, I will ask you questions. In the first side of the T-Chart, you will write down the information that you thought was great. On the second side, you will write down the parts that could use a little more information.*

↪ *Look at the part of the article labeled Behavior. Read the text.*

↪ *Write down information that is helpful in understanding the topic in the first column. Now write down information that is unclear in the second column.*

↪ Give students time to write down their notes.

↪ *Look at the notes you wrote down about this text. Do you think the author did a good job of explaining the text? What changes would you suggest to make it better? (Acknowledge and accept student responses.)*

↪ Go over the remaining tab, Fun Facts, following the example above.

↪ *Let's talk about some of the information you wrote in the T-Chart. How did this information help you evaluate the text? Overall, did you like the text? Explain why or why not? Encourage student discussion, acknowledging and accepting student responses.*

# Extend the learning

Encourage further discussion about the strategy.

↪ *How did evaluating help you as you read this article?*

↪ *Were there parts that you really liked? Why did you like those parts?*

↪ *Reread the information in the article. Do you think the author described the topic well? Why or why not? (Encourage students to use the T-Chart during this activity.)*

↪ Encourage students to practice the strategy with the Related Articles: "Allosaurus" and "Iguanodon."

# Graphic Organizers

# Three Column Chart

| | | |
|---|---|---|
| | | |

Name _____ Date _____

# KWL Chart

Topic _____

| What I Know | What I Want to Know | What I Learned |
|---|---|---|
| | | |

# T-Chart

Name _____ Date _____

# Making Connections Chart

| What is in the text | My connection (text, self, world) |
| --- | --- |
|  |  |
|  |  |
|  |  |
|  |  |
|  |  |

Name _____ Date _____

# Question Words Chart

| What? |
| :--- |
| |

| Who? |
| :--- |
| |

| When? |
| :--- |
| |

| Where? |
| :--- |
| |

| Why? |
| :--- |
| |

Name _____ Date _____

# Making Inferences Chart

Topic _____

| Clues in the Text + | What I Know = | Inference |
|---|---|---|
| | | |

Name _____ Date _____

# Main Idea and Details Sheet

| Main Idea |
|-----------|
|           |

| Detail 1 | Detail 2 | Detail 3 |
|----------|----------|----------|
|          |          |          |

# Venn Diagram

Name _____ Date _____

# Cause and Effect Chain

Cause                                                    Effect

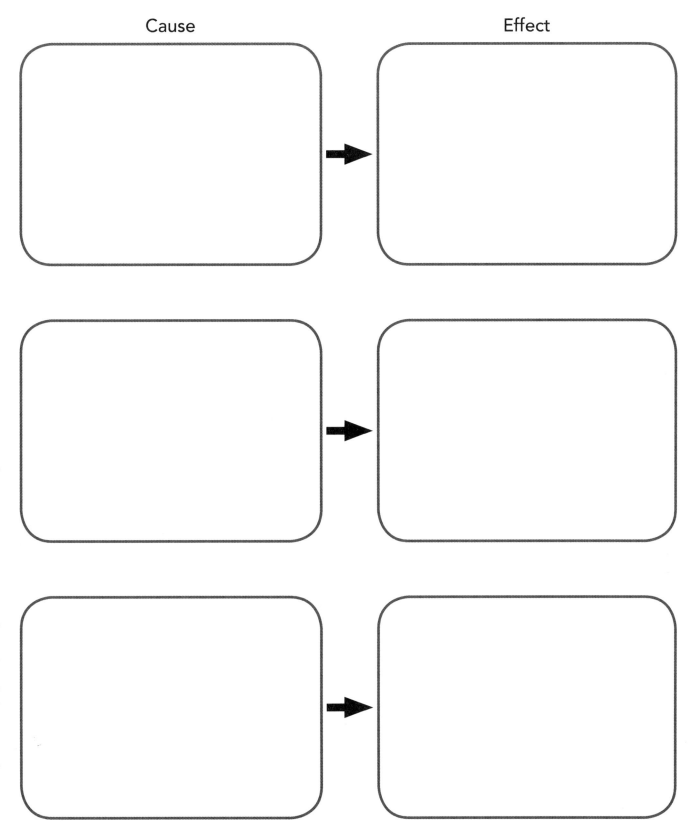

Name _____

Date _____

# Timeline

# Notes

# Notes